We need this conversation to happen. Our bodies are gifts from God, not something to starve, critique, or feel shame over. Jess has catalyzed this needed conversation so beautifully and candidly in *Breaking Free from Body Shame*. Read this book!

JENNIE ALLEN, *New York Times* bestselling author of *Get Out of Your Head* and founder and visionary of IF:Gathering

This is the message we've all waited for. A collective sigh for our souls from the prophetic voice that is Jess Connolly.

KENNESHA BUYCKS, author of *Restoration House*

This book is a generational anthem for women proclaiming all of God's creations are unique, beautiful, and good. It's a heartfelt reminder that our worthiness isn't dependent on a number on the scale. Jess speaks truth and light over the lies and shame we believe about what is accepted as a beautiful body.

REBEKAH LYONS, bestselling author of *Rhythms of Renewal* and *You Are Free*

The most freeing, transformative, and refreshing book I've ever read on the lies we've believed about our bodies and God's truths that will set us free. Filled with grace, humor, and practicality, this is the book our generation needs to crush the enemy's lies and live as the women we were created to be.

HOSANNA WONG, spoken word artist, international speaker, and author of *How (Not) to Save the World*

I've read every book Jess has ever written because, with her love for God expressed in words, freedom rings! Our bodies are banged and bruised by this fallen world as we strive to reach unattainable and ever-changing ideals while the church either remains silent or struggles with what to say. Now more than ever, we desperately need to hear and see the glory of the Lord regarding these good bodies we've been given. In this book, Jess partners with God to he˙

more of heaven. Each chapter is a rope burner, burning away the cords that bind and keep us from living healthy, whole, and free. This book belongs on every kingdom girl's shelf.

ALISA KEETON, founder of Revelation Wellness
and author of *The Wellness Revelation*

If you've ever hated the mirror, felt uncomfortable in your own skin, or complained about the body God has given you, this message is for you. Freedom and a biblical perspective are ours, and Jess leads there courageously and vulnerably through this book.

RUTH CHOU SIMONS, bestselling author of
*Beholding and Becoming* and *GraceLaced*

What an inspired message for women in this generation! *Breaking Free from Body Shame* is a bold war cry against the lies of the enemy that cause us to hide behind our bodies rather than rejoice in our uniqueness. Through her grace-based approach, Jess flips the script on what it means for our bodies to be good, and invites us to name and reclaim who we were made to be.

ALLI WORTHINGTON, author of *Standing Strong: A Woman's
Guide to Overcoming Adversity and Living with Confidence*

In my four decades of living, I've had many conversations with friends about how much we dislike our bodies, what we wish was different about them, and how we want to change things. This book from my friend Jess is a game changer for women. She not only dares us to reclaim what God has named good, but she gives us practical ways to do this. I was challenged to talk about myself differently, I was convicted about the ways I have been consumed with not liking my body, and I was encouraged to speak and think differently from now on. This book is for all women who desire to truly love their bodies because of the simple fact that God created them and called them good.

JAMIE IVEY, bestselling author and host of *The
Happy Hour with Jamie Ivey* podcast

# Breaking Free *from* Body Shame

JESS CONNOLLY

# Breaking Free *from* Body Shame

## DARE TO RECLAIM WHAT GOD HAS NAMED GOOD

ZONDERVAN BOOKS

ZONDERVAN BOOKS

*Breaking Free from Body Shame*
Copyright © 2021 by Jessica Ashleigh Connolly

Requests for information should be addressed to:
Zondervan, *3900 Sparks Dr. SE, Grand Rapids, Michigan 49546*

Zondervan titles may be purchased in bulk for educational, business, fundraising, or sales promotional use. For information, please email SpecialMarkets@Zondervan.com.

ISBN 978-0-310-35259-4 (audio)
ISBN 978-0-310-63661-8 (custom)

Library of Congress Cataloging-in-Publication Data

Names: Connolly, Jess, author.
Title: Breaking free from body shame : dare to reclaim what God has named good / Jess Connolly.
Description: Grand Rapids: Zondervan, 2021. | Summary: "For women who love God but have a love/hate relationship with their bodies, join Jess Connolly to discover a bold new way to rest in God's workmanship and heal the broken beliefs that have held you back from your fullest life"— Provided by publisher.
Identifiers: LCCN 2021000401 (print) | LCCN 2021000402 (ebook) | ISBN 9780310352464 (trade paperback) | ISBN 9780310352501 (ebook) Subjects: LCSH: Body image in women—Religious aspects. | Self-perception—Religious aspects—Christianity.
Classification: LCC BF697.5.B63 C657 2021 (print) | LCC BF697.5.B63 (ebook) | DDC 306.4/613—dc23
LC record available at https://lccn.loc.gov/2021000401
LC ebook record available at https://lccn.loc.gov/2021000402

Published in association with literary agent Jenni Burke of Illuminate Literary Agency, www.illuminateliterary.com.

*Art direction: Curt Diepenhorst*
*Cover illustration: MURRIRA / Shutterstock*
*Interior design: Denise Froehlich*

*Printed in the United States of America*

HB 05.10.2022

*For my mom: Deb Hopper*

*Being made in the image of my Father*
*brought me purpose and healing.*

*That He also made me in your image brings me joy.*

*I love looking and acting more like you as the*
*days pass. Thank you for doing the hard work of*
*breaking free so that so many in our family, for*
*generations to come, could simply step into it.*

# Contents

# Contents

# Foreword

We're all searching for beauty. We're all searching for someone who will see us and know us and love us still. We're all searching for God. If God took on a body to be with us, then our search for Him should, in part, be found in and through our bodies. Yet, as is the case on many journeys to find God, obstacles abound, deception runs deep, and the false versions of what we're really looking for seem to overwhelm us at every turn.

It shouldn't be shocking that in and through our bodies—these avenues of connection with the embodied, incarnate Jesus—we are often met with the diametric opposite of what we seek: we find ugliness, insecurity, isolation, self-hatred, and shame there. Dear ones, these painful experiences don't have to be the summation of the stories of our bodies. In the pages of this book, my friend Jess and many others are bravely leading us toward a different ending, which is really a new beginning.

I first met Jess years ago, probably right around the start of the season of her own renewal and revival that paved the way for this book. The work she and God were doing with her body image at that time overflowed out of her and onto people she encountered. People like me. A major girl crush (on my end) ensued, and a deep friendship grew. She helped me walk away from my shame about beauty before I even knew I needed to, and her hard-won, faith-filled wisdom continues to illuminate the way forward for me and so many others.

When we first met, I was about six years into living with my new body, which is severely disabled. I had always been confident, an extroverted Southern lady and Christian good girl to the core. I was tall and blonde and loud, a haphazard commercial print model and pageant winner, a theatre enthusiast and public speaker. Yet, for as long as I can remember, I was racked with insecurity and shame about my body. Then, out of the blue, as a twenty-six-year old newlywed and young mom, my physical body was decimated by a stroke and a sixteen-hour brain surgery. I awoke to a new reality of major lifelong disabilities—the inability to walk well or drive, double vision, deafness, a frozen vocal cord, a half-paralyzed face, and thick new layers of insecurity and shame.

Yet no matter the depth of our pain or the unique scars we bear, the hope of redemption remains the same. This book has already brought me to hopeful tears of recognition and to a renewed, open-handed posture of release. Jess's words and the stories of other women have reinvigorated my belief that we are being freed, not just despite our bodily struggles, but because of them. This renewal is one of the soul, but it is manifested dazzlingly through our physical selves. The process is as individual as our own beautiful bodies, but the healing is most powerfully done together. Join us. It will be glorious.

*On the journey with you,*

# Katherine Wolf

# A Very Important Disclaimer

Hey, friend.

I want to tell you something incredibly important, now, at the beginning of this conversation: I believe your body has been provoked enough already. One of the definitions of *provoke* is "to stimulate to action," and it's often not beautiful action we're called to but the shame-based instigations and affronts of a world that expects perfection. Our bodies are rarely welcomed into spaces—spiritual, physical, or emotional—where we are allowed and encouraged to be who we already are.

I know that you and I, just by being women who live in this fallen world, have had our bodies named, judged, harmed, and harassed by the enemy of our souls and by other people. I believe healing is found in Jesus Christ, but I do not believe the healing that is ours to access negates the pain any of us has lived through.

Because I believe your body has already been through enough pain, my hope and prayer is that this book will not inflict any more harm on you. My hope and prayer is that you can make it through each chapter without being triggered by language or stories or teaching that leaves you hurting or in shame. My hope and prayer is that this book is a place of understanding and solace, that it is a ginormous light shining toward God, who created us good, redeems every part of our lives, and offers the balm of healing through the power of the Holy Spirit.

For this reason, some of the writing may feel at times more toothless than you were expecting. Some of the personal stories I share may seem mild in comparison to moments you've experienced. It may be that you hear me acknowledge, but not address, some of the more extreme possibilities when it comes to harm that we've caused or that others have inflicted on us. It's not that I don't want to shepherd you through those moments, and it's not that I want to be vague. Rather, I want this book to be safe to read, without you having to potentially relive incredibly painful moments or memories. And I know that while a book is an incredible place to start a conversation and spark an awakening, it will never replace intentional one-on-one, in-person care.

I'm also incredibly aware that my experiences and perspective are just that—mine. They're not comprehensive, they cannot speak for you, and they may not reflect what you've experienced. For that reason, I've invited other women to chime in, so we can get a more expansive view of what it looks like to believe our bodies are good. You'll find their bios in the back of the book. These women represent different races, socioeconomic spaces, and ages, and they have varying perspectives on walking with Jesus. The hope is not that they will speak for you, either, but that we can learn what it sounds like as God speaks through many of us regarding our bodies.

Your body is good. I believe we can stand on that truth because God said it. For that reason, if your body is being harmed—by you or by anyone else—I absolutely encourage you to seek help and healing immediately. Please see the resources section for some places where you can do that.

Here's my promise: I am on your team and in your camp. I believe God is mighty in you, and I believe healing is real. I can't wait to keep breaking free alongside you.

*May grace guide us and vision lead us,*

# Jess

CHAPTER 1

# Why Body Image Is
# a Spiritual Issue

I'm grateful you're here. I believe
healing is available for us. I believe
our culture is ripe for revival as it pertains to seeing our bodies in light of
God's kingdom. I'm literally praying for
you. Let's get started.

I was riding in the back of one of my parents' cars; I can't quite remember which one.

It was the early '90s, and seatbelts felt more
negotiable then, so I was lying down on my left
side, facing the floorboard, which was littered with
kids' road trip materials—coloring books, crayons, a
few small plastic toys. The warm southern sun was beating down on the parts of my body that weren't tucked into the
cloth seats, warming my skin, my cotton t-shirt, and shorts. I was
about to turn nine years old.

We'd just come from a family member's wedding, and it had been *fun*. So fun. I drank virgin strawberry daiquiris and danced the Electric Slide and swam in the hotel pool. My mom let me change into comfy clothes midway through the reception, and I danced for what felt like hours while laughing with my long-lost second or third or fourth cousins. Now, we were headed home, where safety and rhythm lived—the only two things I loved more than virgin strawberry daiquiris and hotel pools.

In the midst of the fun, however, I had made some observations. I had seen the way the other cousins danced in their wedding attire, and I, for some unknown reason, seemed to have been adorned with 10–15 percent more of the skin, of the flesh, than they had.

I don't know why, and I don't know how, but I know it felt wrong.

So while I was safe in the cocoon of the back seat, I took my hand and held it, flexed and straight, like a knife, straining as if it contained the power of prayer, petition, and perfection. I positioned it somewhere between my chest and my right armpit, where the sun was warming the exposed half of my body, and I began deliberately drawing a line down my body.

The line didn't go down the middle, it didn't dissect me in half, but it sliced off the outer ten percent—the extra on the sides of my upper torso, then the soft space on the far end of my stomach, and down my thighs, where there seemed to be a troublesome amount of "leftovers." My hand, an imaginary knife, moved precisely, like a surgeon's tool, down the curviest parts of my body—not with self-harm in mind, but rather as a prayer.

*God—all-powerful and all-able, would you remove this part from me? It seems like extra. It seems not to fit.*

I knew He could do it—I just didn't know if He wanted to.

But I promised God that if He'd remove the unwanted from me, I wouldn't tell anyone—it could be our secret.

I moved my hand slowly down, tracing the track that marked off the areas I'd like to no longer linger and I squeezed my eyes tight, aware of His ability. I was pretty sure if I just looked away and pretended I didn't notice, He would fix me. I promised Him once more that I wouldn't even tell anyone; I'd act like it had never happened.

Afterward, I sat with my eyes still closed, giving Him a moment to move, before I fluttered open my lids and saw . . . I was still me. I was still in my body, which was unchanged. And the car drove on.

It's been almost thirty years since that day, and I have great compassion for that girl who wished she could carve part of her body away. I want to scoop her up and tell her that all of her body is good, that society is into scarcity but God is the giver of abundance. I want to tell her that the best parts of her are her tenacity, her strength, her words, her worship, her motherhood, her sacrifice, her capacity to serve when no one sees. I want to tell her that it's *because* her heavenly Father loves her so much that He denied her request.

I want to tell her that the desire to keep her prayer a secret is the seed of shame that will grow like a weed in her life. I want to tell her that the disappointment she feels over who she is, is a much bigger problem than the extra skin and flesh. I want to tell her that her body is good.

*And yet.*

There is a part of me that knows if I could turn my hand into a knife-shaped prayer of precision and slice off 10 percent of my body today, I'd be tempted to do it. Even now, my secret disappointment and disbelief in the goodness of my own body weighs heavier on me than any extra pounds ever could. I am still that girl. I still need to hear the truth.

And I don't think I'm the only one. I wonder what this story brings to mind for you. Maybe you're questioning your body's goodness as you walk through postpartum recovery, or as you scroll through Instagram, looking at fitness influencers and thinking about the kettle bells gathering dust in your closet. Maybe you work crazy hard at taking care of your body because you have to, because your health is on the line, and you *still* feel the aches and pains of a body fighting disease. Perhaps you go weeks without thinking positively about the skin that you live in, or maybe it's been years.

I have found that my story, though probably not identical to yours, is not far from the collective story many of us carry. Our story is that at some point we believed our bodies weren't good, and we don't know what that has to do with God. Does He care? Does He know? Does He agree? Will He help? What's the plan?

Somewhere along the way, shame became a lens through which we experienced our bodies. Maybe we felt shame for how they were perceived by others negatively—maybe we felt shame and embarrassment for how our bodies were praised. It could be that shame became part of the equation when we couldn't conquer our bodies, when the "problem" of our bodies seemed insurmountable. Many of us might feel like we should be over this, like spiritual and emotional maturity should have enabled us to move past this place by now. And yet we're still out here, all of us, overly exposed to a light that is not warm with grace, but rather judging what is not "right" about us.

Our story is not finished because our flesh is still failing to be all that the physical world expects. Our story is not finished because we are multitudes, and we can believe so many things at once. We can believe the best parts of us are unseen and eternal and still deeply desire for the visible portions of us to be signed off on by the world as OK.

Here's where I'm at today: I live in the now-and-not-yet wrestling match of skin and soul. I know that who I am is loved by God and who I am is still a body, subject to the pain and brokenness and imperfections of a fallen world. I know that the best stories are not always the most simple stories, and there are those who'd like to write off this story, this struggle, as silly or secular. There are those who'd say you can fix this body problem with moving more and eating less, and there are those who'd say the remedy is to stop thinking about our bodies and start thinking about heaven.

And yet here I sit. It's been quite a journey since I prayed in the car at age nine. I have moved much and eaten less. I have read the books and tried the things. I have worn holes in my literal and figurative prayer rugs and dug divots of fervent request in the floors of each home I've lived in since Jesus has been alive in me. I've been shamed and I've been shushed when I speak about my body. I've been praised for how it looks, and I've been pleaded with to stop acknowledging its presence. I've moved, and I've sat still. I've run marathons, and I've watched Netflix marathons accompanied by copious amounts of popcorn. I've gone to conferences, and I've been coached.

I have attacked this sense of my body's not-enough-ness with a secular strategy and with my spirituality, and I am still here, in this body, longing for words that weave a true path to freedom. Not just for myself, but for those fighting alongside me, the genuine warriors of our generation who are asking God,

*Is this a good body? Do You care? Do You agree? Can You help? What's the plan?*

Let's take the opportunity to agree right here and right now: The way we view our bodies is not a shallow, surface issue for the immature or the vain. The way we view our bodies is a deeply spiritual issue because our bodies are made by God, in the image of God, and they are where we encounter God for now. What's more, the belief that body image is just a shallow concern is a lie from the enemy that's wildly effective at making women believe they can disconnect with their bodies to the point of engaging in starvation, harm, and abuse—all because we have agreed that our bodies aren't spiritual. This is a lie we unconsciously use to justify our behavior, and it is so very far from the vision God has for us. Amen?

Perhaps the most essential move we can make in breaking free from body shame is to agree that God cares and wants to walk with us as we learn to love these bodies He made with intention. Maybe the most effective way we can begin this fight against the enemy is to say, "This matters. This is important. This is holy. This is worth talking about."

It's been twenty-eight years and six months since I slid onto my side in the back seat of a sun-warmed secondhand car and wondered if God could or would instantly make me more like the girls around me. As I write this today, it's a dark and slightly chilly night, and I'm on an airplane, with the glow of my laptop warming my eyes rather than the sun on my thighs. But those same particular parts of my legs spread just beneath the armrest because they are still not standard in size. And just above the keyboard, where culture says I'm supposed to cave in, I curve out. And where my head dips down with defiance to type the passionate last few words before the flight attendant says no more, my neck makes an additional chin. Still, I know for sure . . .

*This is a good body. This is a body that can live free from shame.*

And I think of you wherever you're reading this. Maybe in a warm spot in the sun or maybe in the carpool line or even on a treadmill or listening on headphones as you walk. I think about you on your laptop, lounging in your room, and maybe running a soft hand over your own perceived imperfections. I imagine you sitting cross-legged as you move the pages of the e-book with a tap, flipping the pages on the beach, and reading as you prepare to lead others in a group or a Bible study. Even without seeing you, I see you, and I know:

*You are in a good body. You were not meant to live in shame.*

The truest thing about you is that you are made and loved by God. And the truest thing about God is that He cannot make bad things. All of this sounds simple until we own up to the fact that we often want to stifle the very vessels He's placed us in for His glory and for the good of others. If these things are true, why do we struggle to believe them? Why can't we trust the goodness and the *holiness* of the way we have been uniquely made?

This disconnect is what reveals to us that the way we see and experience our bodies is a spiritual issue.

We agree, agree, agree with the premises about His character and the promises of His creation until we bump up against the brokenness we feel about our own bodies.

So while I think it's absolutely permissible and potentially beneficial to ask God the questions you read above, I also believe it's brave to allow Him to ask the following questions of *our* hearts:

Do we believe God makes good things?
Do we know what our bodies are for?
Do we know what makes a body good?
How do we agree with that truth in our daily lives?
Do we want to live free from shame?

That's what this book is dedicated to finding out.

# The Locked Closet in the House of Your Soul

If you grew up going to Christian events in the '90s, you heard this kind of crazy metaphor: *Your soul is like a house, with lots of rooms and doors. Jesus wants to come in and clean up every room.* If you were at a ski retreat or youth beach trip or a revival night, the male speaker with the microphone and the airbrushed T-shirt would begin describing the one room you always tried to keep locked and hidden from God. Maybe you kept a padlock on the door, or maybe you'd even forgotten that it existed, but God wanted to come in (with grace) and tidy that space up.

This illustration usually led to lots of tears and confessions—nobody wanted to be hiding skeletons from Jesus! And yet, thinking back on it now, I (religious studies brain) see how the analogy falls short. I think we produced a lot of teen Christians in the '90s who perceived the best thing they could give God was a tidy house and heart. But Jesus isn't a soft and passive housekeeper and His grace is wild and messy. I don't think His absolute best for us is an Americanized picture of everything in its place. C. S. Lewis said it better than the youth leader with the airbrushed T-shirt:

> Imagine yourself as a living house. God comes in to rebuild that house. At first, perhaps, you can understand what He is doing. He is getting the drains right and stopping the leaks in the roof and so on; you knew that those jobs needed doing and so you are not surprised. But presently He starts knocking the house about in a way that hurts abominably and does not seem to make any sense. What on earth is He up to? The explanation is that He is building quite a different house from the one you thought of—throwing out a new wing here,

putting on an extra floor there, running up towers, making courtyards. You thought you were being made into a decent little cottage: but He is building a palace. He intends to come and live in it Himself.[1]

I often think He wants to knock our houses to the ground and build something new and beautiful. I've seen Him set fire to the house I've built with my own hands, in mercy, so I can start fresh. Sometimes I think living with God is more like carrying a tent on my back and living off the land of His love than living in a house. Sometimes I don't think of myself and God in a house at all, but more like two soldiers running through the forest— Him taking bullets for me and yelling back when I need to duck or turn. When I worship, I picture myself and Jesus on horses together, moving forward in victory and fighting the enemies of defeat and fear and despair.

I don't love the house analogy. But maybe I would if we reframed it.

If your heart was a house, if your life was a house, and the Spirit of God could enter any and every room and bring light, hope, healing, and kingdom-minded wisdom, which room would your body be in?

Let's imagine that finances are a room, our family is a room, our romantic lives are a room, our entertainment is a room (the one with the TV, obviously). Maybe adventure and fun is a room, rest is a room (I'd pick the back porch), and learning or the way you engage your mind is a room (a library, of course). One thing I like about this analogy is that it gives us a moment to evaluate the different areas of our lives and the impact of the gospel on them. Our lives are so much more comprehensive, complex, and

---

1. C. S. Lewis, *Mere Christianity* (New York: Macmillan, 1949).

integrated that my brain can't always process all the things at once. So I appreciate being able to go from room to room and ask, "What impact does God have on this room? What has He done here? Is He allowed? Does this space honor Him?"

## The Problem

Now I'd like to acknowledge the massive problem I see in our current culture as it pertains to women and their bodies. Not only is this a compartmental space, one we often keep from the power and presence of God, but we've made it *just* a room (or a closet) without acknowledging that it may be one of the most *important* places in the house. Our bodies are where we experience our families. Our bodies are where we worship. We use our bodies to serve. Our bodies are where we encounter romance and sex. Our bodies are our main vehicle for rest. Maybe our bodies aren't actually the house; maybe the house is our soul—the vehicle that will transcend our time on earth and eternity even while our bodies change. But the body has to be some integral part of the structure. Maybe the insulation? The drywall? The frame?

Many of us can't ignore our bodies, but we haven't been taught to see them from a kingdom-minded mentality, either, so we live out our lives in a house of the soul—surrounded and encapsulated by confusing messages and broken beliefs.

We're told our bodies are projects to work on, something to present to the world for measuring and evaluating. We're told our bodies are reflections of our righteousness—if we follow God correctly, they'll look a certain way and mirror His majesty and grace. We're told our bodies are trophies—something we can work hard to earn glory, something we can give to those who are associated with us. We're told our bodies are bad, filled with innate and impure longings we should suppress and subdue like hunger, desire, and fatigue.

We are told these messages overtly, subtly, indirectly. We're told these messages from birth, as we listen to our families and leaders and lovers discuss their bodies and ours. We're told these messages in church, from the stage, the screen, and social media. We're told these messages from birth onward, with heightened application around pivotal moments and cornerstones of our life such as graduation, marriage, motherhood, birthdays, vacations, and new seasons.

We've been sold and told a collection of messages about the very container where we experience ourselves, God, His people, and the world. The problem with most of what we've been told is that it's *biblically untrue*. It doesn't line up with the heart, character, and overall message of God and His gospel.

It's not how God would talk to His children or how He has spoken to us about our bodies, but nonetheless, the collection of messages has been delivered by His spokespeople and attributed to His kingdom society.

I believe He is grieved. I believe that the God who created the universe longs for His children—specifically, His daughters—to know the value and beauty and worth He ascribes to their bodies.

I believe there is grace for those of us who have conveyed, agreed with, and passed on these negative messages that negate the work of the gospel in our bodies. I believe we can unravel the lies and untangle the untruths that have kept us contained in a condemnation-centric culture.

I believe there is growth and healing for us on the other side of this. I believe our bodies were made good by a Father who doesn't make mistakes, and I believe that when we begin to apply that truth and administer freedom to the women around us, we'll see renewal in our culture at large.

But we absolutely must turn the lights on, unlock the doors, and be honest about what we think, say, and live into with these beautiful and good bodies of ours.

## Hope and High-Waisted Jeans

Do you remember the first time you encountered someone whose perception of her body was not in line with culture in the best way? The first time you met someone who lived in radical freedom, acceptance, or abundance as it pertains to her body? Did you notice another mother playing hard on the beach with her kids without seeming concerned about her stretch marks? Maybe you took a fitness class from an instructor who didn't fit the stereotype but who never made apologies for her body or let shame take up any space. Maybe while growing up you had a friend who grew quiet when the other girls in your group began criticizing their bodies because she refused to take part in such a ritual.

I regret to say that even now, as I write, I'm scanning my memories, having a hard time picking more than a few people from my past. We could all tell stories of the women and men who had a negative impact on our lives, shocking us with their personal beliefs about the body.

For me, there was the incredibly wise and wild woman who discipled me in college, but who also encouraged me to go on an extremely low-carb diet. Or the pastor who noticed I had gained a significant amount of weight and told me it looked like my heels were going to snap under the pressure of my body. Once, we moved to a church to help a pastor, and the leadership team offered both my husband and me a diet program as a welcome gift. "Thanks for coming to help our church. Please only eat 600 calories a day for the next twenty-one days."

If I'm incredibly honest, most of the truly impactful voices in my life have had this one flaw: *they have neither agreed with nor promoted a kingdom mentality when it comes to the body.* Cultural conformity has been the ideal, and in the worst cases, living up to that ideal has been cast as a form of righteousness. In the bulk of my experiences with others, there hasn't been a desire to break free from shame, either. Rather, shame has been welcomed as a tool to help our bodies continually become better.

*Along came Lily.* Lily was a voice that cut through the crazy to say something true and affirming and wildly encouraging. I was a few years into the process of no longer just accepting my body or even celebrating it, but trying with everything I had to view it in light of God's kingdom. I was trying to grasp that my body was fallen and broken, yet full of potential and promise. I was trying to embrace the body God had given me, and I had definitely begun to give up on ever being anyone else's ideal body type.

And so, one day, I wore high-waisted jeans. Some women with my particular shape may avoid high-waisted jeans or, particularly, high-waisted jeans with a shirt tucked in, which puts your shape on display. It's the old, "I can't wear _____," or "_____ just doesn't look good on my body" argument that many of us live with and throw around. High-waisted jeans with a shirt tucked in "should" be avoided (I'm getting angry just typing that) by women with my body type—but I was over the "shoulds," so I did what I wanted to do.

Lily came over a few days after I'd worn some high-waisted jeans to church. We were catching up on her life and her eventual plans to move to Paris. Lily was so cool. So wild. So in love with God. Just before she left, she looked at me with the beginnings of tears in her eyes and said, "Thanks for wearing high-waisted jeans. Seeing you love your body makes me love my body. Seeing you worship in your body makes me want to worship in my body when I come to church."

I was stunned and blessed beyond measure. At that early point in my own journey, no one had really noticed the outward shifts I was making as my heart changed inwardly. No one had seen my high-waisted jeans as the freedom cry that they were. No one had mirrored back the love I was beginning to allow myself to feel *toward* myself, toward my body. There stood Lily—one of the first harbingers of hope in the battle. It wasn't a lighthearted cry of body positivity, and it wasn't the willful determination to not notice our own figures—it was something deeper and more intentional that she reflected back to me.

It was deep-seated, God-glorifying goodness. Lily saw that I agreed that I was made in the image of God. She saw me naming my thighs and my lower half as a blessing and not a burden. She stood in agreement with me, adopting the freedom for herself as well. Together, for a split second, we were our own community of freedom fighters, sharing this sacred and worshipful agreement: our bodies were good.

I've had that same moment of exhilaration a handful of times since then. I find that even when we're open and comfortable sharing with other women about our bodies, it almost takes a miracle to get to a shared agreement that our bodies are good. We're all on different pages, we have different experiences and stories, and it takes patience and the stripping away of layers of vulnerability to let down our collective guards and make agreements that are rooted in truth.

As precarious as it can be, together is the way forward, conversation is the conduit of this kingdom mentality, and we can start together. Right here. All of us. Today.

## Now Entering the Brave Space

Latasha Morrison, founder of Be the Bridge, was the first person to introduce me to the term "brave space." I've heard the term used in connection to anti-racism work, learning environments, and other avenues of the social justice conversation. Latasha may not have coined the term, but she was the first person to unpack the idea for me, and it has absolutely shifted the way I move into important conversations.

In a safe space, people feel comforted and even comfortable. In a safe space, you can say what's real and true for you without implications or repercussions. The problem with being safe is that while it feels comforting, it's not fertile ground for growth. When we're comfortable, we tend to stay the same.

In a brave space, there is an invitation to be who you are, where you're at, while being offered a challenge and room to grow. In a brave space, you accept the probability that you'll feel uncomfortable, but that your discomfort will be productive. In a brave space, the tenderness and vulnerability you feel is ultimately productive because it leads you to growth.

I perceive that we need to accept the tenets of a brave space in order to press into what God has for us next as it pertains to our bodies. We need to be able to say real and honest things about our bodies, but we also need to step onto ground that is ripe for growth. We need margin to move and expand, to plunge forward into freedom, not stand still where we are.

So here's where we're headed:

We're going to start by talking about what a kingdom-minded mentality looks like in regard to our bodies. We'll look at some of the other positive and negative ideas about the body that are inherent in our culture at large, testing them against the Word of God and looking at them in light of eternity.

We're going to dive into the past and sift through some of the moments wherein we and others have named our bodies against the will and truth of God. We'll ask God for the grace to forgive those who have hurt us, and we'll accept his grace for the ways we've used our words as a weapon against ourselves and others. We'll go back to the original name God gave our bodies as a banner to live under for the rest of our days.

Next, we're going to provide some much-needed rest for our bodies. Maybe not physical rest in the sense that you're used to, but spiritual and emotional space wherein we stop provoking and begin preparing a place where we can repair. Restoration will follow this rest. As we seek restoration, we'll ask *why* we want to grow, and we'll utilize worship as a guide to experience abundance, freedom, and forward movement.

Finally, we'll join one another in pressing into revival. We'll take our place among the throngs of women who are living in liberty as it pertains to their bodies, and we'll use our voices to bring others along with us. We'll use the weight of our freedom to create a wider path and firmer ground for all of us to stand on, and space for all of us to run.

You may notice that we don't talk as much about the shame we feel as we do about the goodness with which we were created. This is intentional because we're going to be replacing lies with truth, trading our chains of condemnation for the certainty that our bodies have worth and value and beauty.

We're going to do all of this in our good bodies. Not just in our minds or in our spirits, but here, where we live, in these tents of flesh that house the Holy Spirit who raised Jesus Christ from the dead. We will join our friend and brother, Jesus, in proclaiming the year of the Lord's favor, binding up the broken-hearted, ushering in freedom for those who are held captive, and providing comfort for all who mourn—here, in our good bodies.

Are you ready?

Together, let's soak in these words about God's heart to proclaim freedom:

> The Spirit of the Sovereign Lord is on me,
>> because the Lord has anointed me
>> to proclaim good news to the poor.
> He has sent me to bind up the brokenhearted,
>> to proclaim freedom for the captives
>> and release from darkness for the prisoners,
> to proclaim the year of the Lord's favor
>> and the day of vengeance of our God,
> to comfort all who mourn,
>> and provide for those who grieve in Zion—
> to bestow on them a crown of beauty
>> instead of ashes,
> the oil of joy
>> instead of mourning,
> and a garment of praise
>> instead of a spirit of despair.
> They will be called oaks of righteousness,
>> a planting of the Lord
>> for the display of his splendor.
>
> They will rebuild the ancient ruins
>> and restore the places long devastated,
> they will renew the ruined cities
>> that have been devastated for generations.
>> (Isaiah 61:1–4)

# Questions

If your heart was a house with many rooms, what room would represent your body? What does that room look like? Is it cared for or hidden? Is it visited often? Is God invited into that room?

What have you been told about your body? List the first three messages that come to mind.

Is there someone in your life who loves her body simply because God made it? How has her friendship or relationship impacted your life?

## Words from Our Friends

**RWP:** *Little me has a similar story to little Jess in that I vividly remember the time when I realized my body wasn't "like" those of others. And I'm still very aware of it. In the thirty years since I realized I don't fit the culture's body standard, I feel I should definitely be finished with what God must be teaching me about contentment. Because that's how it works, right? That has got to be His ultimate goal, or certainly, I would no longer be waiting for that pivotal heart change, or better yet, body change. I feel like what I constantly hear from others in the church is that I'm not experiencing total freedom because I still haven't reached the level of contentment He wants for me. In short, I'm still not quite spiritually mature. But I'm coming to realize that the truth really lies in His desire for me to see my* *body, His creation, as good. To treat it as good. And I'm getting there. He's been opening my eyes and changing my heart, and I'm so thankful to be in this brave space to continue that work.*

Jensine: *Just the other day I was looking at my post-two-kids mom bod and pinching here, sucking in there, wishing away an inch or two at the waist and thighs. The way we perceive our motherhood and these physical vessels that brought life into the world is often out of lack, with the idea that we need to get our pre-baby bodies back, that we are missing out on something as moms. But what a reminder of the God-given abundance in both our life-giving bodies and our mission, that the extra is an overflow of grace so that we can keep giving, giving, giving.*

# CHAPTER 2

# A Better Mindset

Imagine that your body is a story. That every detail, freckle, muscle, movement, and scar tells the story of your life.

Who are the main characters? What are the chapter titles? What themes have unfolded as the story has been told? Have the church and its leaders played a significant role, or have secular voices shaped the way the story has unfolded? Not only is it helpful to trace the source of what we've been told, but also to hold it up into the light and evaluate whether it's true, helpful, lovely, and leads you to love who God made you to be.

So whether the messages you've received about your body are from the church or the wider culture, it's worth asking, "What is true and helpful?" If you haven't kept tabs on what the wider world outside the church has been saying about body image, here's a quick summary. *Let's talk body positivity first.*

# Body Positivity

These are things that make me smile:

At the barre studio where I exercise, there is a mural on the wall. It depicts a group of women moving their bodies. They are all shapes and sizes, and it isn't just some performative set of icons—it's the truth of our studio. Among the members and the instructors, there is no uniform style of "fitness" or "strength." Every body is welcomed and celebrated. This is body positivity at work in the world, and it's remarkable.

I recently heard my daughter singing the lyrics to the song "Let 'Em Say" by Lizzo and Caroline Smith, which bucks the mold of the traditional "model" look to proclaim, "I wanna look like my momma, Five foot two and a natural woman." This is body positivity at work in secular music, and it's beautiful.

Body positivity is more than a hashtag—but goodness, check out the hashtag. In a space that used to unanimously agree that smaller was better, polished and perfect was the goal, and flaws were something to be hidden, there is now freedom where shame abounded. There is now celebration where condemnation reigned. This is body positivity at work in our culture, and it's incredible.

Body positivity might seem relatively new and noisy because of social media (there are over five million posts using the hashtag #bodypositivity on Instagram at the writing of this), but it's an idea that finds its roots in the 1960s. As "free love," feminism, and the Civil Rights Movement were gaining ground, there was also liberty swelling as it pertained to bodies and how we view them.

The term "body positive" was officially coined in 1996 and was in frequent use by the early 2010s. It's an idea that promotes appreciating your body in spite of its flaws, feeling confident in your body, loving yourself, and accepting your body's shape and size. The body positivity movement is why we now see more realistically shaped models in commercials for Dove, Aerie, and almost every mainstream company. Personally, I almost exclusively buy my bras, undies, and bathing suits from Aerie because it's helpful to see how something might look on a body shaped like *mine*. This tactic works. I appreciate it!

But the body positivity movement is more than a tactical tool for brands. It's goodness and truth embedding itself in the hearts and minds of multiple generations who are sick and tired of having shame at the center of the story. It's a wave of inclusivity that, at its best, breaks down previously held perceptions which were rooted in the objectification of our very good bodies. The body positivity movement has been a lifeline for millions, the introduction to a wildly hopeful idea that there's *far* more than one way to be beautiful. I don't know if the person who coined the phrase identifies as a follower of Jesus, but I do know that the idea is in line with His heart for women.

## Body Neutrality

Body neutrality is a term coined in 2010 by a treatment program in Vermont, and I'm incredibly grateful for this language that has helped so many. Body neutrality puts forth the hypothesis that complete positivity is potentially impossible for some, such as those who struggle with body dysmorphia (a condition that keeps someone obsessively focused on the negative aspects of their body which may or may not be visible to others), an eating disorder, a traumatic event that occurred in the body, or even those who live with injuries and disabilities that are difficult to celebrate. I appreciate the body neutrality movement because I have friends for whom it is not easy or even possible to look in the mirror and proclaim love for what they see. Body neutrality makes space for those of us who have deep-rooted frustration, disappointment, and pain related to our flesh.

From a social media perspective, it's not as widespread but is catching on quickly. Body neutrality is a soft place to land, a way forward that is both believable and attainable. It creates space for our hearts to process the pain and disappointment we feel while still throwing off the shame of the overtly negative perspectives we carry.

## The Church's View of the Body

So where does the church stand on body positivity? How does it interpret body neutrality? I'm not far removed from the pulse of the Christian church in America. I speak at two women's ministry events per month around the country for ten months of the year on average. I lead a local church. I am connected with and/or am friends with many mainstream evangelical leaders and pastors. The truth is, nobody is really talking about body positivity. And I've never heard anyone mention body neutrality. The church seems to be largely silent on both outlooks. This is not to say there aren't pastors and leaders who believe in and even embody these tenets. For the most part, though, the concepts have simply not taken root in mainstream evangelical culture. They have neither been preached from our stages nor modeled by our leaders.

I have several theories about why this is the case, but at the root, I see one negative reason and possibly one positive reason. From the negative perspective, I believe *mainstream Christianity tends to be terrified of freedom in our bodies in general*. I wish this weren't true. However, historically, the church has seen body freedom as sinful, and it has tended to dismiss any person or movement that advocates for finding comfort in one's own skin. Freedom is a complex concept that weighs heavily on an individual's ability to listen to the Holy Spirit and determine what is from God and what is not.

My concern is that wherever church leaders cannot clearly communicate boundaries and borders, they avoid an issue altogether. Let me spell this out. The concern seems to be as follows:

If we teach freedom in our bodies, will people overindulge?

If we teach freedom in our bodies, will people wade into alcohol and drug use?

If we teach freedom in our bodies, will those who used to serve faithfully suddenly seek and find rest, leaving the church high and dry?

If we teach freedom in our bodies, will we have to have more conversations about modesty?

If we teach freedom in our bodies, will more people engage in premarital sex?

These are the spoken and unspoken concerns.

Some quick thoughts in response from my perspective:

Don't we already struggle with gluttony in the church?

Don't many people in the church already battle substance abuse, both privately and publicly?

Shouldn't we teach rest to every follower of Jesus, including our high-capacity volunteers and church staff?

Are the rates of premarital sex any lower for those who grow up in the church?

Last serious question—and remember, I'm asking this

of myself, a woman who is wrapped up in this culture to an extreme degree—when did we stop believing grace compels us to change? When did we stop trusting the Holy Spirit to communicate appropriate boundaries through our freedom in Christ? Have we traded the message of freedom for even more bondage because we're scared to let people navigate the complex waters of liberty in their own flesh?

If my hypothesis about this reason for avoiding freedom in our bodies is true, it's wrapped up in a stronghold of fear that needs to be rooted out, both at the individual and corporate level. We will not find freedom and wholeness this side of heaven if our churches and communities teach women, overtly or subtly, to be disdainful of and/or fearful of their own bodies. Such fear contrasts starkly with the love God has for each of us and the fact that He created us in His good image.

Now, here's the good news! I think there is one potentially positive reason we haven't seen the church embrace the idea of body positivity. The concept of body positivity doesn't leave much room for people to lament the pain they experience in their bodies. "Just love your body" is hard for those with injuries, chronic illnesses, and disabilities that hinder everyday living. The gospel, at its core, makes room for lamenting and expressing frustration with the brokenness of the world we live in. The gospel tells us we groan and are burdened in these "tents," and we long for heaven and our resurrected bodies (see 2 Cor. 5:1–5).

You might say that in the Western church, we see something similar to body neutrality, but I'd say it could be more accurately referred to as *body ignorance*. When we overlook the negative ways people feel about and use their bodies, we avoid some sticky situations and some potentially hard conversations. If we pretend everything is fine, that this glaring issue isn't facing us, maybe it will go away?

The problem with body ignorance is that messages about our bodies can still be received and agreed with, and if we don't pay close attention to those messages, they will take root in our lives whether we are conscious of them or not, for better or for worse. Without a strong foundation of truth and freedom, the lies of the enemy still seep into our systematic beliefs about who we are, what we're here for, and what makes us good.

Rather than ignoring our bodies and their significance, I'd rather take this question straight to God: What does He think about our bodies? How would He have us love and treat them? What will happen to our bodies when we die? It's easy for us to act as though the soul is all that matters, like our bodies are merely vessels, but if we're made in the image of God, and He crafted us with intention and artistic excellence, aren't our bodies worth attention? And if so many women (and, I believe, men) are hurting as we hunger to understand the worth of our bodies, shouldn't we be trying to understand the truth of God rather than writing off what feels too complex to grasp?

There's another inherent danger in treating our bodies as though they are subpar compared to our souls. A friend once relayed a story about how her youth pastor referred to his body as "just an earth suit." This dismissal created a vacuum that allowed her to believe it was permissible to treat her body without care, even starving it and abusing it. If it was only an earth suit, if it didn't really matter how she treated it, wasn't she free to manipulate it, even at the cost of her own health? If the body itself doesn't matter, then how can what we do in our bodies matter?

We have so, so much work to do in the church pertaining to viewing our bodies as good. We need a theology that recognizes, responds to, and agrees with the truth of how God made us. We need space for women, specifically, to confess and bring light to this area that is so dark for so many of us, so we can begin fighting shame with fervent truth. And we need instruction about what it looks like to love our bodies because God made them—not worshipping them or idolizing them, but worshipping Him with them.

I thank God genuinely for the healing and freedom the body positivity and body neutrality movements have given those of us who have been exposed to them. But for followers of Jesus who ascribe to His truth, I think there's another frontier to explore.

Body positivity leaves us wanting more in light of the news that eternity is the be-all and end-all for us, and that for now, we are living in the midst of a fallen existence. We can speak positive words toward our bodies while also acknowledging they're broken, that they're subject to the effects of a world that is not God's best-case scenario. What's more, it's not our bodies that we worship or proclaim as perfect as much as it is the God who made our bodies. It's our insistence on *His* power, presence, and glory that leads me to believe my body is good. The statement that I love my body, that I feel positively about it, has so much more *impact* because it's backed up by the belief that the Creator of the universe made it with intention and creativity.

## Let's Glean and Grow

I spent the first two-thirds of my Christian life being in the "spiritual-stuff-only" category, and I can honestly tell you, it wasn't ignorance or pride that drove me to listen to gospel-centered learning. It wasn't that I felt fearful of the world or of experiencing corruption—I'd just spent so long in the dark, I wanted to soak up the light. Now, I've noticed it's become a lot easier for me to listen to and learn from the perspectives of those who wouldn't consider themselves Christ followers. I absolutely believe that God created their minds and can inform their insights with truth, even if they don't claim allegiance to Him.

And yet, as someone who believes that earth is not my final destination, as someone who believes there is something more than just noticing my body or accepting its existence, I can't stop there. I have the freedom to glean from the knowledge of others, to let the light of God's truth shine on that knowledge and illuminate what is real and what isn't, and to continue growing in how I interpret and apply that knowledge.

Fleshed out, this means that we can thank God for the body positivity movement that has bolstered hearts and souls when the church has not. We can take the idea of appreciating our bodies in spite of their flaws, gird that idea with the truth that God made our bodies good and He doesn't make mistakes, apply some grace when our bodies act or feel broken and acknowledge this isn't their final home, and stand next to the body positive gals, smiling and grateful we're in this together.

We can marvel at what He's made like David does in the Psalms:

> When I consider your heavens,
> the work of your fingers,
> the moon and the stars,
> which you have set in place,
> what is mankind that you are mindful of them,
> human beings that you care for them?
>
> You have made them a little lower than the angels
> and crowned them with glory and honor. (Ps. 8:3–5)

We can also thank God for the work of body neutrality, especially those of us who are in Christ and have experienced body trauma or need healing from eating disorders. We can breathe a sigh of relief at the idea that our bodies aren't the most important thing about us. This is a truth we find rooted in Scripture that tells us our souls are what the Father sees, and He died on the cross that they might be united with Him. We can learn from the tactics this movement has proposed and apply them in our everyday lives as we continue unpacking what it means to have a body that has been crucified with Christ.

> I have been crucified with Christ and I no longer live, but Christ lives in me. The life I now live in the body, I live by faith in the Son of God, who loved me and gave himself for me. (Gal. 2:20)

## My Body Lives in the Kingdom

A few years ago, I had a mini awakening about my body. It was late spring, summer was approaching, and I was learning the rhythms of the city I'd been living in for a few years. Growing up, we went to the beach once a year, maybe twice, since it was about four or five hours away. I remember, even then, feeling the dread hit my heart as we'd make the drive—realizing that the next week would mean a lot of bathing suits, a lot of exposed-to-the-light living for my body. I tried not to think too much about the exponential increase of bathing suit time we'd encounter upon moving to Charleston, South Carolina, but it's hard to ignore once you're here.

A few years in, I was getting used to it. Unfortunately, I was also growing accustomed to hearing women talk about how they needed to get ready to be in and be seen in their bathing suits as the summer months approached. One day, I was sitting with a few friends at a coffee shop, and the topic of choice meandered to how we were prepping our bodies for bathing suit season. It's worth noting that, at the time, I was speaking with a few women who were either in college or recently graduated, while I had already rounded the corner past thirty and carried four children in my body.

What I'm saying is, one of these things was not like the others. I'm not sure exactly what question I posed or what conjecture I made, but it was countercultural enough that it stopped the conversation. It may have been as simple as me saying, "I'm not getting my body ready for summer. It's already ready." But after I said whatever I said, all the gals I was talking to looked at me as if I had six heads.

Technically, I was their pastor's wife, and some might have said I was discipling them. We never called it that formally because I learned a lot from them, too. Mostly, we shared our lives, saw each other's strengths and weaknesses, and grew more aware of the goodness of God together. They didn't mind correcting or getting frustrated with me—which was about to be proved by their response to whatever I'd just said.

These gals I loved so dearly looked at me like I was an actual idiot as one of them said, "But we live in AMERICA. This is how it is. This is what is expected of us."

When I replay this moment in my head, I'm proud of my friend for being honest and bold and straightforward. She wasn't challenging me as much as she was acknowledging the very real pressures they all felt. Biblical wisdom can only take us so far when we live *here*, encumbered by the trappings of our culture. But when I replay this moment, I'm also amazed and grateful about the clarity God gave me to respond with a truth I hadn't thought about extensively before, but haven't stopped thinking about since:

"No," I said. "We live in the kingdom. I might live in America, but I *belong* to the kingdom."

To be honest, I had doubts about the words the second they left my mouth. Were they true? Did they mean anything? If they did, what did that change?

It's taken me about five years of turning that sentence—and my subsequent doubts—over in my head, poking and prodding at it, to see if it's really true. I'm thrilled to share where I've landed.

My body is good. God made it with intention and creativity. I believe He knew before the world began what I would look like. The first name that was given to my body by God was definitive: good. I believe He makes good things, and I believe that because He created my body, it is a good creation.

Like all things made by God and held on earth, the body has the possibility to decay, experience pain, and to cause pain—but that first naming still means something. It leaves a desire in my heart for me to get back to a place wherein I treat my body as if it's good and give God glory with that stance. But something wild and infinitely indescribable happened in the year 2000, on the night I accepted the friendship of my Savior, Jesus.

It wasn't just my soul that was claimed for the kingdom of God, but my body, too. I gained a kingdom body with new rights, new freedom, and a new set of cultural values and capacities. How I used my body moving forward wasn't just about the present, about pleasure, or about winning the approval of others. My body was now intrinsically linked to a history that started in the Garden of Eden and would be restored in a future eternity.

## What the Kingdom Means for Our Bodies

The rules are different in the kingdom, mainly because of our King. But let's pull this thread a bit and see what else is true about our bodies because of where we live. Where *is* the kingdom? What's the point of the kingdom? And what does it look like to *thrive* in the kingdom? Knowing these things will help us unpack what a kingdom body is and what it can do.

Here are some of Jesus' words about the kingdom:

> Once, on being asked by the Pharisees when the kingdom of God would come, Jesus replied, "The coming of the kingdom of God is not something that can be observed, nor will people say, 'Here it is,' or 'There it is,' because the kingdom of God is in your midst." (Luke 17:20–21)

Let's start with *where* the kingdom of God is. How can I say I "live" in the kingdom? How can I declare that my body resides physically in the location of the kingdom, as much as or even more than it currently resides in Charleston, South Carolina? Essentially, the kingdom of God is wherever God's Spirit reigns. If you are in Christ, by grace, through faith, you are a part of the kingdom. This is a wildly important truth about *you*. You belong in the kingdom because God brought you in. It made Him happy to do so, and nothing can shake your citizenship in His realm.

That being said, saying our bodies *live* in the kingdom is an important belief for us to grasp because it reminds us that He reigns even over our physical flesh. The body isn't a compartmentalized section of our lives about which we don't need to consult Him, listen to His voice, or seek His wisdom.

Why would I say we live in the kingdom *even more* than we live here in our present earthly space? Well, it's because our physical space is passing away—it's not going to last forever the way the kingdom is. The rules and expectations that our present physical space places on our bodies are constantly shifting, whereas the kingdom's expectations are eternal. The culture of our present physical space says that our bodies are OK one day and not OK the next. We constantly receive messages about our bodies that contradict one another. For example, we're told long hair is in, then short hair is where it's at. We're told curvy bodies are beautiful, but "thinspiration" is everywhere. We're told aging gracefully is good, but we're also sold every potion available to man to slow down the process.

The culture can't make up its mind. While God doesn't waver or change His mind, the cultural messages surrounding us never settle on what is true or good. And as a reminder, there is no one in our current culture who will be unchanging for all eternity. So as real as our earthly reality feels, we have to keep the perspective that the kingdom is also *here*.

The kingdom is now. And the kingdom *comes* when His will is *done*. Is it God's will for me to hate my body, to abuse and accuse it? No. Is it God's will for me to love what He's made, glorify Him with it, and experience restoration, healing, and hope in this body? I believe it is. So here's a twist: not only does *knowing* we live in the kingdom change our mindset regarding our bodies, but agreeing that we *live* in the kingdom makes its power more present here on earth. You don't just get to acknowledge the tenets of a kingdom body mindset; you get to do kingdom *work* when you agree that your body is good. Where is the kingdom? It's wherever God has authority. How does the kingdom come? When the Father's will is fulfilled on earth. We are kingdom women, and agreeing that our bodies have been made good is absolutely His will for our lives—right here and now.

Here's the exciting and adventurous part: agreeing is just the beginning of a kingdom body mindset. Don't get me wrong; agreeing that your body is good will begin a revolutionary process that leads you to restoration and revival, but the initial acknowledgment takes some serious consideration. This is great news because it means we get to experience the exhilaration of healing and hope in this very first step; everything suddenly shifts when we agree our bodies live in the kingdom. But there's even more to come. There's more growth, more exploration, more understanding waiting for those of us who continue to press in.

So let's do just that. Let's keep going.

## An Upside-Down World

So how does one access this incredible kingdom? Through salvation.

So much of the theology about salvation that's widely believed and taught today is rooted in the Old Testament prophetic act of Passover. The first Passover was this great and incredible foreshadowing of Jesus and the power of His blood. The Israelites were in peril and needing rescuing. Moses, their leader, was directed to have them pack quickly and mark the doors of their homes with lamb's blood, as the angel of death was going to move about through the land and would "pass over" those doors marked with the blood of the lamb. Here's a tiny excerpt:

"This is how you are to eat it: with your cloak tucked into your belt, your sandals on your feet and your staff in your hand. Eat it in haste; it is the LORD's Passover.

"On that same night I will pass through Egypt and strike down every firstborn of both people and animals, and I will bring judgment on all the gods of Egypt. I am the LORD. The blood will be a sign for you on the houses where you are, and when I see the blood, I will pass over you. No destructive plague will touch you when I strike Egypt.

"This is a day you are to commemorate; for the generations to come you shall celebrate it as a festival to the LORD—a lasting ordinance." (Ex. 12:11–14)

Fast-forward fifteen hundred years, and we find Jesus, our Messiah, spending His last meal celebrating the Passover with His disciples, then teaching them in His final walk to the Garden of Gethsemane, which would end in His arrest, trial, and crucifixion. First Corinthians 5:7 makes the connection for us, calling Jesus, "our Passover lamb."

For that reason, when I think about the moment of salvation in our lives, I often think about Passover. Time and culture have begged us to reduce salvation into something formulaic and explainable, but it's not. Talk to someone who is fresh in their faith, and they'll confirm this: maybe, one moment, they felt a flood of conviction and hope; maybe it happened over time. For the same reason that Moses didn't hand out diagrams of how exactly to spread the lamb's blood on the doors, I try not to define salvation in terms of exact methods and measurable procedures.

There is often conviction and hope, and sometimes healing. Maybe there is emotion, but there may also be logic and reason involved in seeing the kingdom of God for the first time. Eyes are opened, and ears can hear. There is the ability to respond in obedience, but mostly, there is the wild rush of an untamed God moving in our hearts. Suddenly, we find ourselves living in an upside-down world.

I think about the Israelites a lot. I think about how it would feel to hear the cries of those whose homes had not been passed over. I think about how it would have felt to slip out of their homes with their belongings and their children huddled together, in the middle of the night or the early morning, escaping slavery but also leaving behind any sense of belonging. I wonder how it felt to find themselves provided for in the desert with manna from God, yet long to go back to what they knew, long to go back to normal.

I think about the ever-present hope of the promised land,

and how often they must have doubted its existence. They were the children of God, rescued and held in the midst of peril, but everything about their world turned upside down in a moment's notice.

To be honest, I am wildly comforted when I remember that kingdom living often looks more like the Israelites running for their lives in the desert and less like lapping up American excess. If you tell me I should be living a lavish and enjoyable existence while I wait for heaven, I wonder if I'm doing something wrong. When I think about life before heaven as akin to being provided for in the desert while longing for something else, I know I'm in the right spot.

The "upside-down kingdom" is a phrase popularized by author Donald Kraybill,[1] but I've heard it used so many places and so many times, I've lost count. The phrase speaks to the idea that those of us who follow Jesus find ourselves no longer allegiant to the culture around us—but to the kingdom of God. And His kingdom is so wildly different from our own.

Jesus and the authors of the Bible tell us so much about the kingdom in the New Testament. Here are just a few things we're told:

- God's kingdom is not of this world (John 18:36).
- The kingdom of God is not about eating and drinking, but righteousness + peace + joy (Rom. 14:17).
- Jesus will give us the keys to the kingdom, and our prayers will have power on earth and in heaven (Matt. 16:19).
- The poor in spirit are considered blessed in the kingdom (Matt. 5:3).

---

1. Donald Kraybill, *The Upside Down Kingdom*, (Herald Press, 1978).

- We can't look and see the kingdom because it's in the midst of us (Luke 17:21).
- The kingdom is like a treasure for which we'd want to give everything up (Matt. 13:44).
- The kingdom isn't about talking, but about power (1 Cor. 4:20).
- The meek will inherit the kingdom here on earth (Matt. 5:5).

We're told that Jesus moved from town to town, healing people and talking about the kingdom.

His extensive teaching on the kingdom can't be summed up in this short section, but we can acknowledge one truth Jesus wanted us to grasp: the kingdom of God is nothing like the culture of this earth. It's upside down. It's backward. It's completely different.

You can't purchase or inherit the kingdom the way you can property here on earth. The way you get into it is different—through humility, childlike faith, and allegiance to Jesus. The aim of the kingdom is so wildly different from that of living on earth: the end goal is worshipping God and enjoying Him in eternity, where the aim of earthly culture seems to be making yourself as comfortable as possible *right now* and gaining as much material wealth and excess as you can in order to do so.

If a kingdom mentality means being awake to an eternal focus, centered on glorifying God, and disrupting the bonds of sin, death, and destruction, we're in need of an upside-down view of our bodies. Amen?

As Christians, we understand that Jesus invites us to bring the whole of our lives into the kingdom. So why is it that we tend to leave our bodies out of this equation? Too often, our bodies get left behind under the assumption that they are more "of this world" and less spiritual than the next? Yet our bodies are meant for the kingdom.

## Kingdom Body Mindset

The cornerstone of a kingdom mindset is in the first four letters of the phrase. If we're residents of a kingdom, we have a king. The king makes the rules; the king sets the cultural tone. In our case, the King created the kingdom and all it inhabits for His purposes and pleasure. The King is in charge, and we've got to know Him to understand what it's like to live in His kingdom.

Our King leads in love. Our King has a good plan and is committed to serving His people. In fact, He doesn't call his people servants, but friends. Even more than that, He names them as His children and ambassadors, giving them access to all that He has and the capacity to act on His behalf. He is good and forgiving, slow to anger, and always merciful. He's also good and just; He doesn't turn a blind eye to pain or brokenness—rather, He is always engaging in rescue and redemption.

Having a king doesn't automatically ensure safety or blessing or easy living. But having a good King, a kind King, a loving King—a King who is willing to give His life for your freedom? That's a different story. Because we live in a kingdom where our King is also our Creator and Savior, the way we view the bodies we live in within this kingdom shifts. Your King loves your body because He made it, in His image, for His glory. Your King loves your body, not because it's a tool with which He can get His work done, but because it's a treasure where His Spirit is housed here on earth. Your King loves your body and gave His life so that you might experience Him in your body here and now and see your body restored in eternity.

Your body lives in a kingdom presided over by a very good

King. And that impacts and affects how we live and move every single day.

With that in mind, let's ask some probing questions: What do you think God thinks about your body? What do you perceive is God's stance toward you, as a whole person, in this very moment? If you and God sat down to have a conversation about your body, your image, what do you think He would say about it?

I perceive that we need a moment of unraveling right here (at least, I always need one), and we probably will need it over and over again. I have to separate the God who created me and the fallible humans who have spoken for Him in my life. I have to separate the good, gracious, intentional Father from those who have volunteered to be His spokespeople. We often need to untwist and untangle the truths about our King's view of our bodies from lies that have been spoken by those who claim to love His kingdom, or by those who mean well but don't yet understand the kingdom truth about their own bodies.

In this book, we'll talk about renaming and what it looks like to experience healing—and even restoration—after we acknowledge how others have named our bodies. But for now, let's go straight to the words of our King (the Bible) and ask ourselves, *Do I perceive and receive Him in the right light? Or have I ascribed assumptions and attitudes to God that were never His to begin with?* Here's what *He* says about our bodies:

> So God created mankind in his own image, in the image
> of God he created them; male and female he created them.
> (Gen. 1:27)

How does God feel about your body image? Well, He made you in *His* image, so I'd say He feels great. I mean that. I believe God loves you, and He loves your body. Even if you've "let yourself go" in the world's eyes. Even if you've done harm to your body; even if it's injured or altered. What's more, I don't think the King of our kingdom is capable of *not* loving your body, or He would cease to be God.

While God is not limited, there are things He simply won't do because they're against His character. For example, God can't hate His own image or those He made in it. Technically, He could do anything, but God is true to Himself and His Word, and He simply will not act in any way that is not in accord with His revealed character traits of love, perfection, and faithfulness.

Your body image is the perception you have of your body. What's wild is that when God looks at your body, He sees Himself. When He looks at you, He sees His own goodness and glory. And you need to know that God loves His image. God cannot see you without seeing Himself, and when He sees Himself, He sees glory.

There's a handful of questions I'm tempted to answer for you, but for those of us who are in Christ Jesus, I believe the Holy Spirit and the Word of God to be better communicators than I ever could be.

So as we consider these questions about your King and His perception of you, can I send you to a few places in Scripture and allow God to do the talking?

In Ephesians, we hear about how He crafted us with foresight and intention:

For we are God's handiwork, created in Christ Jesus to do good works, which God prepared in advance for us to do. (Eph. 2:10)

In Psalm 139, we're reminded that He intricately created us. He doesn't just see us, but made us with love and affection:

> Oh yes, you shaped me first inside, then out;
> you formed me in my mother's womb.
> I thank you, High God—you're breathtaking!
> Body and soul, I am marvelously made!
> I worship in adoration—what a creation!
> You know me inside and out,
> you know every bone in my body;
> You know exactly how I was made, bit by bit,
> how I was sculpted from nothing into something.
> (Ps. 139:13–16 MSG)

First Corinthians calls us to remember that our body is more than just an earth-suit or a profane place outside of His presence:

> Or didn't you realize that your body is a sacred place, the place of the Holy Spirit? (1 Cor. 6:19 MSG)

Here's where the kingdom body mindset gets powerful, with more *oomph* than any cultural norm or expectation: In the kingdom, *you* are not the one naming your body good; it's not *your* thought repeated over and over again until you believe yourself. You're taking your cues and following the Father who created the universe. We're no longer lone survivors standing up to a wicked world that's telling us we're busted. We're not in a bad dream, trying to scream, but no sound is coming out.

The deafening roar of the Lion of Judah is breaking chains of shame, darkness, and defeat with this proclamation of protection over His beloved: "This is My daughter. I made her body good, in My image. Let no one say otherwise. Her body is good."

# Questions

What body image movements have
you been exposed to?

Which of these has been a blessing? What has
helped you to form a positive body image?

How does it make you feel to know that
God is not neutral about your body?

Do you agree that mainstream Christian
culture has shied away from these
messages? Why do you think that is?

What's your immediate response to the idea
that your body lives in the kingdom?

What would it look like to live as if the
kingdom is real in your body today?

## Words from Our Friends

Sarah: *Growing up in purity culture, I was taught that
my body was bad. It wasn't something to be talked about, and it
definitely wasn't something to love and honor. It wasn't until
physical therapy school that I took a Pilates for Rehab class and
heard the teacher say multiple times, "Thank your body for
being so strong. Look what your body can do." While we
were learning about how to use Pilates in rehab, we were*

*also learning how to affirm and appreciate our bodies for what they could do. I started seeing my body with gratitude that it could walk and run and give hugs and encouragement to friends. It allowed me to see potential and life in places where I previously saw death. Now, when I'm having a bad body image day, I physically list out the things my body can do and thank God for those things. Sometimes the list is just that my body got me out of bed, and sometimes it's that I was able to lift a heavier weight, but it has changed my perspective to be able to thank God for the things he made my body to do instead of focusing on the way it looks.*

**Jillana:** *The gospel, at its core, makes room for lamenting and expressing frustration with the brokenness of the world we live in. The gospel tells us that we groan and are burdened in these "tents" and we long for heaven and our resurrection bodies (see 2 Cor. 5:4). This is relieving news because we can let go of the idol of fitness and the idea of the perfect body. I am never going to have a perfect body here. The sooner I can make peace with that, the sooner I can focus on getting fit in order to be healthy and to serve God well, while looking forward to the day when my body will be effortlessly perfect in every way.*

CHAPTER 3

# Renaming What the World Has Labeled Less-Than

Confession—I own too many domains, as in website domain names. A few years ago, I figured out that if I had a good idea, for a business, a book, or a ministry, I should absolutely buy the domain, or at least see if it's available before I take a step further. The problem is, sometimes I forget about the idea, and then I end up paying $11.99 a year to "hold" the domain name. For example, one time I bought the website "iworkwithmodels.com" because a bunch of my coworkers came into work wearing really cute outfits. I thought maybe I'd start a fashion blog where I showcased their cute styles. I still own the website, but have not gotten around to doing anything with it.

Part of my work with Go + Tell Gals, the organization I run, is helping women step into their God-given call to coach others. A few nights ago, I was working with a group of said coaches, and I had a website idea: coachesareworthit.com! We could start a whole marketing campaign around why it's so great to work with a coach. I went to buy and it and discovered it was already taken. Who else would buy coachesareworthit.com? I went to another website where I could investigate the ownership of said domain and found something hilarious.

I am the owner.

I'd already bought it.

I love naming things. I love picking names for websites, for businesses, for babies. If you need a kid or a book named, I'm your girl. Let's get a whiteboard and a Bible and a thesaurus and go to town. For this reason, my children love to hear the stories of how they were named.

Elias was a name gifted to us by a family we admired. They had two grown daughters, we were having our first son, and they had always wished they could use the name Elias. Benjamin, our third child and second son, was named Benjamin after we heard one of our favorite preachers explain why he'd named his son Benjamin. It means "son of my right hand," and we never wanted Benjamin to feel second or third but rather near and close and important to us. Cannon, our baby, who is now seven, was perhaps the easiest to name of all our children. I had a difficult pregnancy, involving complications and bedrest. One time, in the middle of a really stressful ultrasound, I just said the name, "Cannon Connolly" aloud. It just came, and it was the rock we needed to stand on, a hope to see him face-to-face.

Gloriana Eloise is our second-born child and first daughter. Her name tells a story of heartache and hope. She was originally going to be Talitha Katherine Connolly—Tali Kate or Talitha Kate. My husband and I bickered over the pronunciation of

Talitha, but it's an Aramaic word used in Mark 5 when Jesus raises a little girl from the dead. He says, "Talitha koum," which means "Little girl, get up." I'd loved this account from Mark ever since I was a new follower of Jesus, and I had always planned to name a daughter Talitha.

And then came her twenty-week ultrasound. I knew in my gut she was a girl, but the wand and the gel and the screen confirmed it. The ultrasound technician measured and measured and measured with her head cocked slightly to the left, as if something wasn't quite correct. We were told our baby looked a little small, but not to worry. They'd run a few extra tests and get back to us. Glory's story is long and beautiful and redemptive (and I'd love to tell you the whole thing another time), but to sum it up, a week later, we were faced with the potential of losing our beautiful baby girl for the first of many times. My husband, Nick, and I prayed; our family prayed; the community rallied around us and prayed; and in the midst of that time, I knew I couldn't name her Talitha. Maybe I didn't have enough faith? I'm not sure. But I knew I couldn't name her after a story where Jesus raised a little girl from the dead if that wasn't going to be her story.

We decided then to call her Gloriana, meaning Glory Born, because surely she would be—one way or another. A few weeks later, more tests were run, and in one shocking phone call we were told we had a healthy baby. It was almost more jarring to drop our concern for her than it was to pick it up in the first place, but we moved forward in gratitude. The name Gloriana stayed.

I'm also a renamer, and I have no shame about that. I've personally gone from Jessica to Jessie to Jessi to Jess over the span of thirty-six years, my name changing with age and life season, always becoming a little bit more aware of who God has made me to be, always trying to step into that with more intention. I often say that there are people who call me Jessi because it's familiar and familial—this means they knew me before we started churches or wrote books. But there are also people who call me Jessi, and it feels heavy, like they're suggesting they know who I really am because they know who I used to be. It feels as if they're calling me Jessi because they don't want me to grow.

We changed our old business's name twice, once because we wanted to, and once because we had to. We changed the name of our church from Gospel Community to Bright City. We felt like Gospel Community was who we were, and Bright City was who God was asking us to be. In the biblical narrative, renaming was far more common than it is now, and I appreciate that.

Abram and Sarai became Abraham and Sarah, agreeing with their new names that they would no longer be barren but the mother and father of generations.

Jacob became Israel, and in so doing, he went from identifying as a trickster to someone who honestly wrestles with and acknowledges the Lord's power in his life.

Simon was renamed Peter (which means "rock") by Jesus, a name that carried weight and position in the new church of early believers—especially poignant to remember the name was given to him even though Jesus knew Peter would betray him. He told Peter, "On this rock, I will build my church" (Matt. 16:18), giving him a new position and new responsibility.

Saul became Paul, marking a life transition that saw him shift from a persecutor of Christians to the man who would write the bulk of the New Testament.

Of course, not all names are created equal. These are all examples of names that were bestowed on the recipient with great love, names that were carefully considered and selected to speak *significance* over a person's life.

Lesser names are spoken over us all the time with no such intention—labels, accusations, even nicknames. While some names are designed to lift us up, others are designed to drag us down. And I want you to hear me on this: the truth is, we get to choose which names we agree with. There is a wildly beautiful power in giving a soul the option to agree or disagree with the label, description, projection, or perception of worth a name gives them.

I'm not advocating that we all run to the Social Security office and give ourselves new legal names, but we've been given the opportunity to pause and ask: *Do I consent to the meaning of my name? Do I agree with the weight of the nicknames I've had attributed to me or that I've accepted from others? Am I actively participating in naming (things, other people, myself) in a life-giving way?* And of course, we should all ask, what name have we given our bodies?

Do you call your body great? Weird? Awkward? Have you named yourself as strong or weak, unique or basic? In the past, have you ascribed to yourself the label of pale, short, curvy, messy? These are more than just labels or descriptions, especially when we hold on to them and live under them as if they're truth. We treat these words as if they're no big deal, but we know that names are absolutely important, so let's treat them as such.

## The Name That Hurt

If we were together right now, my body might get unusually still, and I'd try to lock eyes with you without making it weird. If I could tell you're a toucher, I might grab your hands. If close contact is too much for you, I may move further away. What I'm saying is this: I'd do anything in my physical power to make sure we both seized the next few moments for all they're worth.

The misnaming that has occurred in our lives has been a large part of our wounding, and I believe, in Jesus' name, going back to the first name we were given can be healing.

The names that we and others have given our bodies has

been the foundational trauma that many of us are still trying to overcome. The misnaming has been the weapon that brings continual injury to our most vulnerable identity. The misnaming has come from people we love, people we hate, people we know, and people we don't. The misnaming has come from our own lips and from the megaphone of a culture that cares very little for our souls and very much about our compliance. The misnaming of our bodies has left every single one of us feeling flawed, even when our minds know a truth that says otherwise.

My gut tells me that the memories of our misnaming are close for us, even if we haven't thought about them in years. My spirit tells me we may have forgotten the words or the people who delivered them, but the wounds and fears have stayed with us all the same. And my mind knows that even the names we tried not to agree with, even the ones we tried to cast off, made an impact on us and left us limping to some degree.

I wish we didn't have to give the misnaming we've all experienced even one second of airtime. I wish we could shake our heads and shake off the devastation and injury those past moments incurred. But an assailant so damaging cannot be ignored, and the injuries absolutely won't heal with time if we don't address them head-on. We are a wounded people, and if it's healing we want, it's our pain we must pay attention to, at least long enough to call it what it is and ask for help from the right place. The amazing news is that giving attention to misnaming doesn't inherently give it more power if we know in the end we have access to the power of renaming.

My heart aches as a mother, a daughter, and a friend to say the following words: our negative naming most likely started at home. Someone you loved and trusted and needed named your body or theirs in a way that forever framed your worth. Your mother told you she didn't love her body and that was alarming to you. Your father said you were too heavy for a piggyback ride. The elders in your family openly critiqued or praised your body in a way that made you feel wildly uncomfortable. Your brother or sister casually mentioned some flaw of yours, and you'll never forget it. These were not necessarily bad people. In most cases, it was likely our deep love and trust of them that caused us such confusion and pain when they said these things.

It breaks me to say that for many of us, the pain and the words were much more overt and oppressive than those I've just described. And I am so sorry for any misnaming that happened to you at home. I think of the first misnaming, the one that most likely happened at home for many of us, like the first bite of the tree of the knowledge of good and evil:

The serpent was clever, more clever than any wild animal God had made. He spoke to the Woman: "Do I understand that God told you not to eat from any tree in the garden?"

The Woman said to the serpent, "Not at all. We can eat from the trees in the garden. It's only about the tree in the middle of the garden that God said, 'Don't eat from it; don't even touch it or you'll die.'"

The serpent told the Woman, "You won't die. God knows that the moment you eat from that tree, you'll see what's really going on. You'll be just like God, knowing everything, ranging all the way from good to evil."

When the Woman saw that the tree looked like good eating and realized what she would get out of it—she'd know everything!—she took and ate the fruit and then gave some to her husband, and he ate.

Immediately the two of them did "see what's really going on"—saw themselves naked! They sewed fig leaves together as makeshift clothes for themselves. (Genesis 3:1–7 MSG)

Did you catch that? The serpent's misnaming was incredibly sneaky *because it was so subtle*. He whispered into Eve's ear, saying *if* you do this one thing, *then* you'll be like God—and in so doing, he named her as lacking: *Eve, you're not enough as you are. You're not like God.* Talk about a masterful lie—the first few chapters of Genesis proclaim the glory of man and woman as made in the very image of God!

What God proclaimed as *very good*, the serpent declared *not enough*.

We can see what came next: shame. The first time Eve was misnamed was the first time she was introduced to shame. That's what shame does: it whispers to us that we lack, and suddenly we are aware of how "less-than" we are in the eyes of others. We didn't know, and then suddenly, we did. Just as Eve was unaware of her nakedness, then suddenly ashamed of her natural state, when we believe a misnaming spoken over us, we are thrust into a whole new reality that does not agree with the kingdom truth about our bodies. Like Eve, the knowing that came from the misnaming didn't help us; it harmed us. And we couldn't unhear or unsee a world once we were exposed—shame and striving were suddenly that much closer to our skins and our souls.

For many of us, this kind of naming also occurred at school, perhaps at recess or in the cafeteria. These were the first moments we heard another human use piercing words to name our bodies. For me, it was as simple as the other girls starting a "gymnastics club" on the playground. They told me I couldn't be in it because I was too heavy to lift myself over the bar. They were right, and suddenly, I felt so wrong. I started a running club with a few boys instead, and I wonder now how long I've been subconsciously trying to outrun that moment.

The initial misnaming may have happened for you via TV, and it may have occurred later, when you assumed you'd go through life unscathed. It may not have impacted you until marriage or after your first child was born. It may have been a coach, a dance instructor, a youth pastor, a boyfriend. It may have been someone you never personally knew. I have a distinct memory of passing a boy in the hallway in high school—I have no recollection of his face or identity—and hearing him mention with disdain the arms of another girl I knew, then instinctively assessing that mine were bigger than hers. It was a misnaming, by a faceless human who held no density in my destiny, that I have not forgotten for over eighteen years.

The misnaming we experienced told us we were too big or too small. The misnaming told us to be wary of becoming certain things. The misnaming told us we were abnormal or ordinary. The misnaming happened in the natural, a transaction of irreverent and obscene words in which we exchanged our ability to hear with our ability to believe we were made good in a heaping moment that we could not have possibly consented to.

The misnaming is worth mourning. The misnaming is worthy of our attention. It cannot be reversed, but it can become a moment reclaimed. With a wild mix of mercy, grace, and healing (that we absolutely have access to), we can be women who take off the brokenness of the names we've been called and pick up the beauty of the true names we've been given by God.

## A Moment of Mercy

Maybe you can recall the first time words were used to describe your body or describe another person's body. Maybe you can remember the first moment wherein you felt the covering of security become stripped away and the shame, disappointment, or fear rushed in to envelop you. If you do, or if another poignant memory comes to mind, can I invite you to spend just a few moments there with me? I don't want to linger for the sake of morbid introspection, but rather because 2 Corinthians 12:9 says that His power is made perfect in our weaknesses, and I don't want to miss an ounce of the power we have access to in this area of our lives.

Another reason I want to entreat you to keep going with me, even back to the place where the hurt or confusion may have begun, is because our hero is waiting there for us. In the movies, he rushes in when the peril is at its peak, when the villain's monologue is at its zenith and the vulnerable victim is in the most need. What's different for us is that our hero was *always* ready and already walking with us. He didn't need to hurry or hide until the last minute.

I know that Jesus Christ probably did not appear to you in the flesh the first time someone came for your body in a negative way. (If He did, I want to hear that story, and you'd better believe I'll trust you!) But I do believe that our Hero, our Father, the Creator of the universe was not turning a blind eye at the origin of our unrest as it pertains to how we were made.

I believe we can trust His promises to us.

Let's look at some of the good promises our Father makes:

> God doesn't miss a thing—
>> he's alert to good and evil alike. (Prov. 15:3 MSG)

> The Lord will watch over your coming and going
>> both now and forevermore. (Ps. 121:8)

> "Don't be afraid, I've redeemed you.
> I've called your name. You're mine.
> When you're in over your head, I'll be there with you.
> When you're in rough waters, you will not go down.

> When you're between a rock and a hard place,
>> it won't be a dead end—
> Because I am GOD, your personal God,
>> The Holy of Israel, your Savior." (Isa. 43:2–3 MSG)

Blessed be the God and Father of our Lord Jesus Christ, the Father of mercies and God of all comfort, who comforts us in all our affliction, so that we may be able to comfort those who are in any affliction, with the comfort with which we ourselves are comforted by God. (2 Cor. 1:3–4 ESV)

He was there. What's more, I believe He was grieved. The child He loved and created with intention, holiness, beauty, and care was about to be misnamed by another human who could never grasp the pain and confusion they were ushering in.

I believe He was there. I believe He was full of love, compassion, mercy, and deep grief for you.

I had a friend who experienced incredible trauma when one of her children almost died. Later, she went to a prayer ministry where the woman praying with her asked her to replay the event, picturing where Jesus was throughout every moment of the trauma based on what she knew of His character.

When she replayed the event in her mind, she saw Him holding her, holding her child, His face full of mercy and compassion and care. He was concerned, but not flustered, He was moved to mercy.

Since my friend told me about her experience, I've tried to do the same thing with the tense or terrifying moments in my life. And I'm inviting you into that practice.

Knowing our God is full of justice and truth, knowing He crafted your body in your mother's womb, knowing He loves you and He'd leave His entire flock just to come and get you, where do you suppose Jesus was at the moment of your misnaming?

How did His face look? Where were His arms? Do you think that maybe, in His compassionate all-knowing power, there's a possibility He thought about and prayed for *this* moment in the midst of *that* one, eagerly anticipating the restoration and redemption you'd experience?

I'm asking you a set of incredibly intentional questions about your soul: Do you believe God loves you and cares for you? Do you believe He has mercy and compassion for you in your weakest moments? Do you think He grieves the way your body has been named, by you and others?

I do. I do. And I do.

The God who is full of mercy toward you was absolutely there when you were misnamed. He was broken over the burden being placed on you, and He was already setting a plan in motion so that this wound would be healed and could be used in your life for the good of others and for His glory.

I am not thankful for the moments when my body was named with unholy words and an iniquitous identity was attached to me based on how I looked or did not look. I am not thankful for those moments. But I *am* wildly thankful that God was there, holding me in compassion. And I am thankful He's here now, bringing restoration and redemption when I need it most.

This, right now, is another moment of mercy. And His compassion and care are ours to receive if we want them.

## The Enemy Is the Enemy

As we're sitting in the tension of that first naming—or any subsequent one that comes to mind—let's think about the villain, the enemy in that moment. Who said the hurtful thing, whether directed at you or themselves or someone else? If you knew them, how did it impact the way you loved them and felt loved by them from then on? Did it seem like maybe it ruined your relationship?

Was distrust brought into the mix? Were you shocked to hear that person demean another person or maybe even themselves?

Now I'm wondering if you've ever been complicit in any naming. Either your body or someone else's? Either in front of them or behind their backs? Have you ever used your words to speak death, defeat, and defection into the flesh God formed with intention and care?

My guess is yes. My sad, convicted answer for myself is also yes. So what do we do when we're all complicit in negative naming? When we've all been the bad guy at some point? How do we move forward in a way that is kingdom-minded but also honors our hurt and makes us accountable for the hurt we've caused?

I don't believe we should sweep all occasions of naming under the rug and give those who have injured us blanket absolution. I am, however, advocating that we remember that the enemy of our souls is the true enemy in these situations. Remembering this helps us fight the right assailant, forgive ourselves for the negative namings of the past, and access healing in a more complete way. Here's what Scripture reminds us about the actual enemy and how Jesus differs from him:

> "The thief comes only to steal and kill and destroy; I have come that they may have life, and have it to the full." (John 10:10)

When I remember that I've been a part of the horrible phenomenon of naming our bodies outside of the good boundaries God created and sustained us in, it's easier for me to have compassion on those who have done the same to me or around me.

When I remember that the enemy of my soul is the author of

lies, the one who wants us to run from the truth of God, it's easier for me to experience the mercy of Christ and want the same for others. When I remember that every soul who has made the horrific mistake of naming a body in a negative way was subject to this fallen world and the propaganda it promotes in regard to creation, it's easier for me to forgive. It's easier for me to remember that Satan is the enemy.

I have forgiven some people who used their words to name my body but will never speak to them again. The forgiveness is because of Jesus, but it is *for* me, so I don't grow bitter, so I allow the truth of the good news of Jesus Christ to have its way in my life. But I don't have to continue to be in a relationship with those people in order for forgiveness be complete. That wouldn't be healthy or lead to my wholeness.

I have forgiven and am still in relationships with other people who used their words to name my body or theirs in a heartbreaking way. I have learned how to use my own words to break ties with the negativity most of them still speak even as they're saying it. I have forgiven them in the past, have compassion for them in the present, yet refuse to allow their words to rest on my soul, spirit, or body. We'll talk more about what this looks like in practice later on.

Allowing the enemy to be my enemy, instead of the human who has misnamed me, does not negate my pain. But allowing the enemy to be the enemy does not give unsafe words from other people a free pass to wreak havoc in my life. Allowing the enemy to be my enemy does not mean that I never tell people when and how they've hurt me so we can both hopefully grow. Remembering the enemy is the enemy does help me humbly remember my own need for the gospel, while providing the proper direction for my anger. I am angry and broken and busted over the misnaming of bodies that has occurred and is occurring in our culture. I am angry and broken and busted over the number of women (and men) who have experienced years of pain or bondage from the weight of words spoken over them.

But my active anger is directed at the enemy of our souls, because I believe he is the author of lies, and thus, the origin of the conflict. My anger is also directed at him because I've been told how to fight him and combat his advances without holding back. In fact, I've been commanded and equipped to demolish the strongholds he wants to introduce into my life, and so have you.

Maybe the thing that makes me the most angry about the enemy and the misnaming he attempts in our lives is that it's an attempt to usurp our God-given family heritage. Our Father is a namer at the core of His character, and we've been given the advantageous authority to name people and things in a life-giving way by our adoption into His family. This capacity for naming things good is a kingdom-given-gift that is our legacy, and we've got to take it back from the petty thief who thinks he is running the show.

## A Namer and a Giver

Let's move on from the enemy and pay attention to the Father and what He was up to in the incredible moments of creation. Join me in Genesis:

> So God created mankind in his own image,
> in the image of God he created them;
> male and female he created them.

God blessed them and said to them, "Be fruitful and increase in number; fill the earth and subdue it. Rule over the fish in the sea and the birds in the sky and over every living creature that moves on the ground."

Then God said, "I give you every seed-bearing plant on the face of the whole earth and every tree that has fruit with seed in it. They will be yours for food. And to all the beasts of the earth and all the birds in the sky and all the creatures that move along the ground—everything that has the breath of life in it—I give every green plant for food." And it was so.

God saw all that he had made, and it was very good. And there was evening, and there was morning—the sixth day. (Gen. 1:27–31)

I've said it before, and I'll say it again: I'd be so grateful if we could see a replay of creation in heaven. Wouldn't that be amazing? Imagine, one day on the new earth, a smiling Jesus passes out tickets to some Grand Canyon-sized amphitheater. I can't wait. We've got a 4D theater at the aquarium here in Charleston, and my kids and I love to go. It's four-dimensional because it's actually a 3D movie with smells and light movement. Sometimes, if it's a movie about whales or something, they'll spray you with water at just the right moment. It sounds nuts, but it's awesome.

I imagine the eternal amphitheater would be even crazier than that. Maybe we'd be suddenly walking in the garden, noticing the soil teeming or the waters still brewing from being parted. I'll tell you what I'd pay attention to: the face of the Father when He created them. Scripture tells us that the triune God was on hand at creation, and He said, "Let *us* make mankind in *our image*" (Gen. 1:26). Was the Spirit sending colors bursting all around like kinetic fireworks? Was Jesus kneeling nearby? I imagine them all smiling—maybe something more than a smile. But I don't have to imagine pleasure, joy, and even divine delight in the work of His hand.

He made light with the His Word and called it good. He made darkness and called it good. He made land and water, plants, the sun and moon, and then animals—and He called it all good. God, our Father, wasn't surprised at His own craftsmanship or capability. There wasn't a chance it was going to be bad. And yet, each and every time, He used the same breath he used to create to then confess and confirm the *goodness* of what He'd made.

But then He made people, and something shifted.

The Hebrew word for "very" in Genesis 1:31 is potentially my favorite word in the entire Hebrew language. It's the same word that means "very" when God tells Joshua to be *very* courageous in Joshua 1:7. The word is מְאֹד, or *meod*, and it means "muchness." Muchness good. He stood back, saw what He had made and said, "This is muchness good."

He made you with His word, declared His creation good with the same, and He keeps going with us and the words. He keeps speaking affirmation and life and worth into us and over us through the power of His Word. It's like He can't get enough of us, of talking to us.

He called us good with His Word.
He gives us His Word when we don't know what to say
   (Rom. 8:26).
He accomplishes what He wants in our lives through His
   Word (Isa. 55:11).
He tells us what's next with His Word (John 16:13).
He lets us in on secrets with His Word (Jer. 33:3).
He's going to end the fight forever with His Word
   (Rev. 12:10).

Our life with God is crafted with the words He continually speaks to us, over us, and through us. It was started with words, and it's sustained by His Word. He speaks, and the earth is held. He speaks, and grace goes forth. He speaks, and creation comes to life. He speaks, and value is ascribed.

He's a talker, but not in such a way that His words lose value with increased volume. Every word of His is perfect, measured, true, just, right, real, and incredibly significant.

You can trust His voice more than any other. And He called you good. He called you *muchness good*. He was the one who first named you. He grieved when the world called or calls you otherwise, and it's His Word that will put us back together and send us out in our healing.

Naming is our God's right as Creator. Naming is our God's game as Redeemer. Naming is how He denotes worth, direction, and value. Naming is how He reminds us of His promises and practices.

The question we must ask ourselves is this: Whose voice will we long for and listen to? Whose label will we accept and live into? Which naming will we allow to define us?

What's in a name? And which ones will we choose to respond to? Which will we choose to reject?

Let's not answer this question too quickly. The easy response would be, "God's—of course!" We could then move on as if it's that simple, as if it solves everything. Rather, I believe it's a weighty question that's worthy of our time. Throughout this book, we're going to look at a handful of labels that have been assigned to our bodies, and I'm going to ask us to genuinely consider, do we want to accept what culture has ascribed, or work against the status quo to agree with God's Word and what He's spoken?

Each moment is going to take careful consideration and examination of our hearts, but our healing and the hope of living free is up for grabs. I believe it will be absolutely worth our while to consider what He's said as opposed to what we've been misnamed.

When you consent to a name, you consent to being known by the Namer. When we consent to the name God has given us, it's even more powerful because we're acknowledging that we also *belong* to Him.

> Now the LORD God had formed out of the ground all the wild animals and all the birds in the sky. He brought them to the man to see what he would name them; and whatever the man called each living creature, that was its name. So the man gave names to all the livestock, the birds in the sky and all the wild animals. (Gen. 2:19–20)

The very first job man was given was naming, proof that our Father was taking this whole "made in our image" business very seriously. What He does, we are made able to do. What's more— what He does, we are invited and commanded to do. Think it was just in the garden? No, let's pop over to Proverbs:

> From the fruit of their mouth a person's stomach is filled;
>> with the harvest of their lips they are satisfied.
> The tongue has the power of life and death,
>> and those who love it will eat its fruit. (vv. 18:20–21)

What if part of the healing that is ours for the taking is found in the going and the naming? What if our participation in turning the tide of our culture is where we'll find our ultimate freedom? What if using our words to build a world where other women believe God's truth about their bodies is what will actually help us believe it ourselves?

What if naming is also our responsibility, but we're shirking it because we haven't realized what's at stake? What if we have the answer to what ails a generation tucked in our hearts, our phones, our pockets, our purses by way of our Bibles? What if the truth and Word of God, given to us as ambassadors, is the healing balm creation is crying out for?

What if we are the namers, set free to speak life, to bring this message to the people who need it most: "Your body is good."

## Questions

What do you think about when you think of your own name? How do you describe yourself?

What negative occurrence of naming comes first to mind?

What kind of name-giver do you want to be known as?

# Words from Our Friends

**Tiffany:** *Growing up, I always shared my name with at least one other classmate. This was true up until I entered optometry school at twenty-three. Because I have always shared my name, when naming my kids, I, like Jess, have been very intentional about choosing their names. I look for names that don't land on the popular baby names lists. I search for names with depth and rich meanings, and I often pray for them to grow in character based on those meanings. We were made by a God who not only created us in His image, but* *called His creation very good. Just as I want my children to remember who they are based on the names I have given them, God wants us to remember who He says we are, even when it comes to this earthly tent. His words "very good," were not isolated to our social-emotional aspects of being, but applicable to our whole persons. We cannot allow the enemy to convince us that we are "Tiffany with the big legs and bum," as I was referred to growing up, and we also cannot be participants in identifying people as anything other than who God says they are. God gave man the authority to name things, and our words carry weight. I want to choose words that lighten, rather than add to what is an already heavy burden for many.*

RWP: *For as long as I can remember, the adults in my life talked about their weight and need to be on a diet. Whether words about dieting were spoken directly to me or just in my presence, it definitely shaped my thinking. "Skinny" was another word for healthy. Not long after my third child was born, I'd been talking a lot about "diet food" and wanting to lose that baby weight! At one point, my oldest, who was four at the time, just started crying and said, "Mommy, I don't want you to die!" I quickly realized that, to his little ears, diet and die sound an awful lot alike. It was a wake-up call that he was hearing the same things I remembered hearing. But it only hit me a few years later, once I was in my mid-thirties, that dieting wasn't the default space I wanted to live in for the rest of my life. I could change the narrative. I could change the way I had used "healthy" and "skinny" interchangeably. I can name things as I see them now, not the way I saw them as a confused child. I can be a name-giver who is grounded in HIS truth.*

**Kim:** *I am muchness good. I didn't realize I needed to hear that. I am MUCHNESS GOOD. I have broken ties with names I have been called in my lifetime, but I can't recall a specific name someone else has called me that relates to my body. The one thing I do know is that I have called myself plenty of names. And even if I haven't called other people names out loud, I can admit that I have done it in my mind. I have also been complicit in conversations with other women in name-calling in relation to the body. I want to be a change agent, to be part of the good naming of a generation desperate for healing. I want to speak life and release freedom to the captives. I want to be known for that.*

# CHAPTER 4

# Your Body Does Not Belong to the World

I've heard of people doing weird things on Ambien, the sleeping pill. Some people Ambien-eat or Ambien-email. This wasn't that.

I did send the email in the middle of the night, but it wasn't pharmaceutically induced. I think I was just desperate. Something must have happened as I slept, something that illuminated just how frenzied my soul felt. Who knows where I got her email address or what that first message even said. I think I just brazenly begged for her help.

I'd emailed Alisa Keeton, founder and director of Revelation Wellness, and told her that I was desperate for some shift in my body and the way I viewed it. I was fed up with how it looked, but I was also exasperated by how I *felt*—not physically, but spiritually. I was in my pain profoundly. I was at the end of myself.

I asked her if she'd coach me in my health and fitness journey, because I needed help.

The very next day, she replied and said yes—but she wanted to know she'd have access to my heart in the process as well. More than that, she wanted *God* to have access to my heart.

We started a mentoring relationship that week. She walked me through the program she had developed for people to get and stay free, which involved a ton of spiritual work. The physical work just followed where our hearts were. The first week, the workouts I was doing were intimidating and left me sore, but by the third and fourth week, I was moving in liberty and enjoying finding out how much truth I could stretch into as my body took on new challenges as well. I experienced wild freedom under Alisa's care. I can't thank God enough for what He did in that season.

When we finished several weeks of intensive one-on-one coaching, Alisa and I stayed friends. She sent me out, sent me on to keep ringing my freedom bell with my body. Sometimes she'd text me and ask, "Are you still on the freedom train?" Sometimes I'd tell her it was dragging me; sometimes I'd tell her I was riding on top of it screaming for everyone else to get on. Anyone who has experienced years of abusing their body knows you can agree with freedom in your brain but not feel it in your bones. Sometimes I felt free, but after my work with Alisa, I always *knew* I was free, and that made all the difference.

The freer I felt, the freer I acted. When I started working with Alisa, I was occasionally exercising, maybe running a little. I had never felt super fit or athletic, but God was rewriting and renaming my body, and suddenly, this new world was open to me. I couldn't get enough of it. Moving was no longer a punishment or a moment in my day that left me wallowing in shame. I felt at home in my skin, not because of how it looked, but because I was spending so much time connected to my body. Endorphins were flooding through me, and I was accessing the God-given desire to eat food that was good for me. I joined a gym, I trained for half-marathons, I did off-the-wall workouts like aerial yoga, where I hung from silk strings attached to the ceiling. When you don't know you're free, you don't hang from silk strings attached to the ceiling, you know? Everything was changing, and Alisa got to bear witness to it up close and personal.

As the freedom train rolled on, I hit a small bump. OK, it was a medium-sized bump. Work was picking up, my kids needed me more as they grew, and my life balance got a little wonky. I was in the thick of finishing my first book, still exercising every day, running a small business and our local church when my body had a mini-crash. I found myself in the hospital with meningitis, truly so blessed not to be sicker than I was, but with a road of recovery in front of me. Then, the meningitis/hospital stay/influx of medicines in my system set off a series of alarms in my flesh, my autoimmune disease flared up, and I began to develop infections in various parts of my body. In the midst of this, I gained a significant amount of weight in a short amount of time.

My particular autoimmune disease is Hashimoto's, which attacks the thyroid. I was diagnosed with it in 2008, and I've had seasons when it was more of an inconvenience and seasons when it was difficult to manage. The more minor symptoms are feeling cold and fatigued, and having a hard time losing weight. But the more serious symptoms are on the immunocompromised side; when I get sick, I get *really* sick. For a few years in a row, I got pneumonia when everyone else got colds. So when I got meningitis, I got *really* sick. Everything just started breaking in my body, which was especially frustrating in light of the health victory I had been living in.

My heart was on the freedom train, but my flesh was faltering and experiencing pain. It was a tricky season, but I was grateful for the truth tucked into my heart.

In the midst of all that, I began to see a new trainer who worked with women with autoimmune diseases, and her program *truly* helped me begin to experience some healing. We cut out all the foods that aggravated my illness, and I did less cardio and more weight lifting since it was better for my adrenal system. I rested more, dry brushed my skin, and drank my water. My body quickly began responding to these shifts. I was so grateful. I was working hard, loving my body well with every intentional morsel that entered it, and trying with everything I had to move forward in patience and gentleness since she (my body) had been through so much.

The trainer I was seeing had her own body image issues, and we occasionally talked about them. I had already begun to stand firm about the goodness of my own flesh, but it was still a tender topic at the time.

There's never a "good" source to hear bad news from, but it's particularly painful when a misnaming comes from someone who is leading you. In this case, it was my trainer. I'd trusted her to guide me; I'd assumed that because she was a believer and a compassionate woman, she'd work from the same set of truths I did. But as I was about to discover, she was on her own journey related to loving her body as God's good creation.

Alisa had coached me to affirm my body as I moved it, to agree with God's naming especially when I *felt* weak. She'd even coached me to affirm my body as I tried on clothing in a dressing room, never letting a tender moment become ground for the enemy to tear my heart up.

But my trainer didn't have the same insight and wisdom Alisa did. This was honestly understandable, as I'm not sure anyone on earth has as much wisdom and insight as Alisa. It's with compassion and grace that I can tell you I completely forgive my trainer for what she said next. I know it was a mistake, and what the enemy meant for harm I believe God has and will use for good.

We were in the midst of a hard workout, me moving with every ounce of effort I had, and to distract me, she was catching me up on her own body image woes. I think I was doing squats with an annoyingly heavy bar.

She had recently gained weight, and it was discouraging her, she told me.

I did another squat. I was barely paying attention.

She was actually going to begin meeting with another trainer to help her get the weight off, she said.

I did another squat.

That's when she looked at me and, with tears in her eyes, said, "Jess—I only weigh about ten pounds less than *you* right now, and it's so upsetting."

In that moment, I dropped the bar.

I took a deep breath and summoned every ounce of strength I could find in my body as I stepped slowly toward her. She'd been looking the other way and glanced at me in surprise, ready to tell me to go back to squatting.

I had to speak the truth.

"My body is good," I said, "It's not a marker of badness. Please don't compare yourself to me in a way that's negative ever again."

She wasn't defensive, but nodded as I spoke, with tears in her eyes, her face flushed with what I'm assuming was embarrassment. She was and is a child of God who loves and serves other women, and I know her intention was not to hurt me. She apologized.

The rest of the workout was a little tense, but we both made it through the full hour we'd scheduled. I walked to my car, and instinctively, called Alisa. I was in tears. It was a lot like that first email—I didn't really know I was reaching out to her until I heard her voice on the other end of the line. And that's when I experienced one of the most miraculous phone calls I'll ever remember.

I don't think Alisa even said hello. She just started talking when she picked up the phone. "God told me you'd be calling," she said. "He told me to tell you your body is good, and no one gets to say otherwise. He told me He loves you, and you're doing great. Your body is good. I'm so sorry that happened. Your body is good."

To this day, I've never told her the full story. I haven't needed to. We both remember that phone call with fondness—me because it absolutely cemented my belief that God loves and cares for me intimately, and Alisa because it was another chance to utilize her gifting and ability to hear from Him.

But even more than for that phone call, I'm incredibly thankful for what it taught me: the world will not be kind to my body, and therefore, it doesn't get to speak into it.

## Accept or Reject

We're big into agreement in the Connolly household. Not agreement as in, "everyone has to get along," but agreement in the sense that you confirm and hold on to what's being spoken to you. If we're instructing our kids, we'll often have them repeat back what we're saying so we're sure they agree. Even if we're just speaking encouragement to one another, we might repeat it and say, "Hey! Rub that in!" while physically rubbing their chest or back.

A few years ago, Nick preached a sermon series called "I

Agree," and he used the illustration of the little legal documents that pop up on our phones and computers when we download a new app or sign up for something new.

These agreements are usually legally binding, but if we're honest, we don't read them. We just scroll, scroll, scroll to the bottom and hit "Agree." In Nick's sermon series, he addressed how many of us do the equivalent in our spiritual lives. We flip through the Bible or sit through a bunch of sermons and say "Agree, agree, agree" without really receiving the weight of what we've been told.

It's a gift for us to remember that when it comes to the names our bodies receive from others, we have the powerful capacity to agree or disagree. We have the right to accept or decline.

There are a handful of settings in which we may feel less capable of breaking free and accepting or declining certain agreements. Those settings make this practice less straightforward, so let's address them first. Simply put, it's difficult for a kid to disagree with their parents when they're young and things are spoken about their body, their person, their value, and their life. If you didn't have the words to reject something a family member spoke over your body when you were an adolescent, there's no shame in that. There is only compassion and care from a good Father who would never have spoken like that to you.

Such words can be devastating, whether they were direct and evil words spoken against you or a more subtle wounding of words that came occasionally. It could have been a nickname or an inference, a comparison or a long string of cutdowns. Whatever or however the words were presented, the truth remains: children have an incredibly hard time rejecting the lies and unkind words of adults who have authority over them. And those early moments can often leave them feeling unable to fight the misnaming that comes from others for years to come.

But here's the thing: from a kingdom mindset, children don't "belong" to their parents. They are entrusted to their parents, but they are the Lord's. Even legally, we call children "dependents," not property. A parent does not have authority to supersede the name God has already given their child. And if God has named anyone good, let no one say otherwise.

This isn't a parenting book. But I'll tell you that my personal conviction is that it is my calling as a parent to listen to God and mirror His heart back to each of my children. This takes prayer and effort to pause and hear His heart for each of them. I have to be incredibly careful about my words so as not to put burdens on them that He wouldn't.

Do I do this wrong? Yes. A lot. Do all of us do this wrong with all types of people? Yes. A lot.

We talked in the last chapter about trying to see misnamings through a lens of empathy and potentially, even, forgiveness. But as we move forward, it's important to note how situations in our past may have weakened our own perceived power to agree or disagree with what was spoken over us.

If you couldn't reject the early misnaming, do you feel unable to do it now? Do you still have a hard time shaking off the unkind things your parents or those in authority spoke to you and over you? For those of us who struggle with that, I don't believe it's because we're weak—I believe it's because we're tender and pliable, the way God made us. But I do believe we can heal and establish new boundaries, growing new muscles that enable us to reject any ungodly words spoken over us.

As we begin to break some chains and some ties with the lies that have come our way, with the names that have been wrongly spoken over us, with the authority others have taken unjustly in our lives, here are three truths to anchor you when misnaming comes your way.

## 1. Words Hold Whatever Power We Give Them

This truth can feel out of reach for children or those who are vulnerable to submission and authority. But many of us now have the space and authority to at least begin rejecting messages from those who are not in authority positions over us, and we can ask God to heal the wounds of our past. This takes time, and for many of us it may take help from a counselor or a pastor. I also believe it will take prayer.

> You have as little to fear from an undeserved curse
> as from the dart of a wren or the swoop of a swallow.
> (Prov. 26:2 MSG)

I love this verse from Proverbs. An undeserved curse, a negative name that we don't allow to permeate into our souls can be obnoxious and annoying without being destructive and deadly. Right off the bat, I entreat you to see any damaging words from anyone you don't belong to as a really frustrating bird. Yes, it might fly in your face temporarily, but it is never going to take you out. You are much stronger than it ever could be.

## 2. You May Have to Remove Yourself from the Space Where the Words Are Spoken

This is a little trickier. Again, there are countless situations wherein this may not be possible. You may be in long-term relationships with those who don't use their words in God's way. You may be in work situations with those who participate in misnaming. But many of us *willingly* place ourselves in communities where speaking about our bodies negatively is normal and acceptable. In those cases, we are volunteering to belong, but we don't have to.

You can walk away from a conversation wherein anyone's

body is being disparaged. You can use your voice to change the conversation. You can choose to no longer surround yourself with people who have such conversations if, after using your voice, they refuse to stop misnaming others.

There are many situations wherein we cannot control what is spoken over us and must go to God to help us rename what has been bruised. But often it's as simple as saying, "I no longer belong here."

## 3. We Have to Remember Who We Belong To

We won't have the tenacity, boldness, or faith to respond to any of these situations if we don't have a clear kingdom-minded mentality. Your body is not the world's, but whose *is* it? We touched a little on this in chapter 2, but let's revisit the basics for emphasis and clarity.

Many of us may need to shake off disturbed feelings when we talk about belonging to the kingdom and family of God. So let's remember here that our Father is a kind, good, benevolent King—who doesn't *need* us to do His work or His bidding, because He is all powerful. He doesn't want to dictate what happens in our bodies. He's so pro-freedom, He created us, purchased freedom for us with the cross of Christ, and gave us the opportunity to live and worship and respond to Him how we choose.

> It is for freedom that Christ has set us free. Stand firm, then, and do not let yourselves be burdened again by a yoke of slavery. (Gal. 5:1)

Galatians tells us that God doesn't give us freedom so that we'll love Him more or so that we'll do what He wants us to do. God wants our freedom just because freedom is good. And He wants us to have every good thing in abundance through Him.

And we know that in all things God works for the good of those who love him, who have been called according to his purpose. (Rom. 8:28)

Romans tells us that when we belong to God, He is always working out the details of our lives for *our good*. He uses harm for healing, He allows pain to produce something in us. He has our best interest at heart.

Belonging to God is nothing like belonging to a human, even the very best human there is, because a human can't love or lead or treat us the way He can.

The more time we spend thinking about what it means to be a woman who lives in the kingdom, who is defined and named by her King, the more uncomfortable we'll get with belonging to the world and being labeled by it. The more time we spend learning about our kingdom rights and the capacities given to us through the power that raised Jesus Christ from the dead, the less we'll care about meeting the expectations of the world.

How do we fight comparison, breaking the chains and avoiding the traps our culture has placed all around us? We know and speak the truth about who we are, Who we belong to, and what that means for our lives.

## Put It into Practice

It's transformative and powerful to look at your body and agree that God made it good. Hope and healing spring up when we remember the moments when our bodies have been named unkindly and partner with the Spirit of God to *rename* them good. But you want to talk about world-changing, freedom-fighting, warrior princess-type behavior? Look at the world and say, "This body was never yours to weigh in on in the first place."

To end this section, I'm going to invite you into a few questions and practices that may help you remain in the brave space of renaming.

**First, some hard questions:**

1. *How much media do you consume on a daily basis that glorifies an "ideal body"?* Remember, the amplification of an ideal body is almost always subtle.

    For me, this has been one of the most meaningful shifts in my movement toward agreeing with a kingdom body mindset. I didn't realize how desensitized I'd become toward images that asserted a standard level of beauty, or one that we could all at least aspire to reach one day.

    Removing the media I was voluntarily signing up for (shows, magazines, certain Instagram accounts) gave my mind and soul a little more space to access the strength I needed to continually name my own body as good.

2. *What do you think it would look like for you to agree and act like your body belongs to God?* Later we'll talk about worship as a path to restoration in our bodies, but it's good for all of us to get in the mindset of asking ourselves this question. For each of us, naming our body as good looks different in application and throwing off any allegiance to the world will also look different. What does it look like for you? What action steps would that involve?

3. *How often do you willingly consent to conversations about bodies (anyone's) where the undertone is negative, critical, or overtly evil?* This is as simple as talking about your thighs with your friend at the pool or as destructive as defaming someone else's body right to their face. Either way, as women who are made in the image of God and believe

our bodies reside in the kingdom, this kind of talk has to go.

**I suggest a few quick steps for changing this pattern in your life:**

1. *Ask God to convict your heart.* Many of us may have allowed this in our lives for so long, or we may have been taught it by example from such an early age, that we can't even hear it anymore. Ask God to make you feel wildly uncomfortable anytime you participate in a negative conversation about anyone's body.

2. *Take the grace, leave the shame.* Jesus Christ defeated sin, death, and shame on the cross. Take the grace that compels you to keep growing, and leave behind any shame that constricts you.

3. *Remove yourself from any environment of misnaming.* Especially if you find yourself in relationships or cultures where this kind of talk is prevalent, there will be an immediate temptation to correct others. I've found that sometimes, the most powerful and productive correction is my lack of complicity. If women I know and love begin talking about their bodies, I don't rebuke them. Instead, without huffing or puffing, I simply walk away. I don't want to be complicit in this.

   If certain gatherings or friend groups always seem to advocate for, adhere to, and gather people with the same ideal body beliefs, I stop spending time in their presence. If someone I'm following on social media consistently glorifies or defames their own body, I unfollow. We have the freedom to say, "This isn't safe or wise for me to consume." You'll soon see I'm not advocating for silence in the face of sin, but I would encourage all of us to know that oftentimes, we can massively shift the culture around us just by not cosigning on what is being discussed.

4. *Finally, when the time feels right, speak the truth in love.* One of the simplest ways I began speaking truth in love to my sisters is by saying, "Please don't talk about my friend like that." If someone I loved critiqued their own body, I'd say, "Please don't talk about my friend like that."

   Often, just speaking truth and goodness over my own body is revolutionary and shifts a conversation. I also have the capacity to speak with love, mercy, and grace, and to tell others, "This conversation isn't how our Father would talk about us or others. Please, let's be more cautious."

   I trust you'll find your voice and the best ways you can change the conversation when needed. I trust the Holy Spirit to give you the words, the compassion, and the bravery to boldly declare, "I don't belong to the world. I refuse to talk about or treat anyone's body in this way."

## Now, let's try some life-giving practices:

1. *At vulnerable moments this week, I encourage you to speak truth and life over your body.* When you're exercising, changing clothes, getting ready in front of a mirror, or feeling insecure in any way, speak *truth*.

   If these statements can be backed up by Scripture, with the authority of God's voice and Word, even better. You'll know they're not just empty phrases you're pulling out of nowhere.

   Here are some examples:
   - This body is good. (Gen. 1:31).
   - I carry the peace of God in my body (Phil. 4:7).
   - This body is a temple of the Holy Spirit (1 Cor. 6:19).
   - My body is worthy and valuable to God (Isa. 43:4).

- I was created with intention, purpose, and creativity (Ps. 139:13–16).
- I have the mind of Christ (1 Cor. 2:16).

2. *Spend time in prayer talking to God about your body.* It's a simple but profound practice. Get brutally honest and bring all the negative names you're struggling with to His feet. As you pray, don't feel like you have to measure your words or make sure they're perfect. Tell God how you feel about your body. Ask God how He feels about your body. Ask Him to give you a vision for what kingdom work He wants to do in and through you.

3. *Make a short list that entails what you love about your body or what you love that your body can do.* Try to focus on what *you* love, not what the culture approves of or others have complimented. Fight the defeat. Make the list—even if it's small things. Do you love that your body can bring comfort to your children? Do you appreciate how tall you are or how strong your legs are? Do you love the way your fingers type quickly or the way your ears enable you to listen to others with compassion? What do you love?

I want to leave you with the reminder that you are powerful because you are made in the image of God, given freedom and agency to lead yourself and others. I want to remind you that the Spirit that raised Jesus Christ from the dead is alive and at work in you. Your body is not up for debate or critique by the world, but instead, you have been given the capacity to make decisions about how you move, who you surround yourself with, and how you worship God with your body.

We break free from body shame by daring to actively agree that we don't have to keep going in the broken systems of this world. Your body is good. God said so. End of story. Let's believe it with our whole lives.

# Words from Our Friends

**Treasure:** *What do I love about my body? This may be the strangest answer, but I have a mole on my nose that I absolutely adore. I love how it mirrors the look of a nose ring. It makes me feel unique. It's a small feature, but every time I look in the mirror, I thank God for it. I feel beautiful with this mole. Besides that, I love how small my hands are. I feel sophisticated when I get my nails done. Something as simple as my nails and hands makes me feel important. We all have our quirks, and these are just some of the things I love about my body.*

**Kati:** *I'm forty-seven years old and still working through this. My dad passed away when I was twelve, but in the short time he was in my life, he did serious damage. He couldn't accept that I was a girl and that I had a disability. He'd spank me every time I'd fall down, saying I wasn't trying hard enough. He'd yell at me because I couldn't balance a two-wheeled bicycle. At gatherings with his family, I was either too thin or too fat; my hair was too long, too short, too curly, or too straight. I was never good enough for them. When I was a teen, his mother told me I was damaged goods and would never amount to anything. My mother's family was the polar opposite and always my safe place, but it seems that the negative things have more impact. They led me to unwise decisions* regarding my body and relationships. For years, I lived with an "I'll show you" mentality, and it affected my relationship with them and with others. I did eventually come to forgive them—mostly—reconciling myself to the fact that they loved me the only way they knew how. But I'm still working on that as the layers keep peeling back, and I'm recognizing the enemy's role in my life even then.

# CHAPTER 5

# Resting from the Quest for a "Better" Body

He was smiling when he said it. Like he was doing me a favor. This boy had the brightest of teeth, and they were gleaming when he said it. Don't ask me his name or how we were acquainted, but I could tell you everything else about the moment. It was a warm afternoon during the fall of my high school freshman year. I was walking to dance practice after school, bag flung over my right shoulder, headed to the track to meet the team I'd eventually get kicked off (bad grades will get you every time).

I swear to you, I remember feeling the need to restrain myself from taking my bag and slamming him in the nether regions with it. Just to reciprocate some of the pain he'd just slammed into my heart.

*"A few of the guys and I were talking, and we think you'd be just as pretty as your sister if you lost about twenty pounds."*

Again, he was smiling as he said it, teeth gleaming. He had no reason to believe it was inappropriate to say.

So now I want to go back and give his mom a hug, or maybe his sisters. I want to find him on Facebook and check in on his wife and make sure he doesn't ever say stuff like that to her. Because if you can deliver that kind of one-liner to a girl you barely know, smiling like you're giving her a gift, your words forever implanting themselves in her heart—I can only imagine what kind of heart damage you'd walk around doing.

But then I remember that I was fourteen, while he was not much older, and I pray that God has grabbed his heart and slowed his tongue. I remember that I've said worse to myself and others. I remember that he learned that behavior somewhere and probably needed some healing himself.

I knew my sister was beautiful; I wasn't blind. I knew she was beloved and esteemed in our school. I remember feeling warmth and gratitude, not just jealousy, for who she was even before I met Jesus, and those good feelings have only grown exponentially since then. It's just that no one had ever compared us so explicitly, and no one had ever phrased it in that exact wording: the attainability of that goal was suddenly on the table. But it wasn't a goal I'd ever held in the past.

It wasn't the first time or the last time someone would speak a deficiency over my body.

If you fixed your teeth . . . (you'll be less distracting).

If you lose any more weight . . . (your face will look weird).

If you tone up your arms . . . (I'll take this one: I could hit you harder for saying this?).

If you got Botox . . . (you'd book more churches that use
 HD cameras).
If you got a boob job . . . (no one would know, but your
 clothes would fit better).

And so on and so forth. I know we could all add line after
damaging line to the list of things we've been told would make
our bodies more presentable and prepared. But I'm here now,
pulling the biggest lever you can imagine, screaming *Stop!*, and
asking a few questions:

1. What in the world are we getting our bodies ready for?
2. Who is deciding what is acceptable?
3. When will we ever be enough?

Before we go any further, I'd like to make a wild proposition:
If you do nothing else, your body is good. If you do nothing else,
your body is good. If you do nothing else, your body is good.

I know it may not *feel* good. I know the effects of this
fallen world may have left it injured, sick, or functioning less
than perfectly. But here's the thing: I often think that much of
our disappointment with our bodies comes from an inadequate
understanding of the purpose of our bodies *and* a misplaced
understanding of our ultimate destination.

Let's look at this passage from 2 Corinthians:

So we're not giving up. How could we! Even though on the
outside it often looks like things are falling apart on us, on the
inside, where God is making new life, not a day goes by without his unfolding grace. These hard times are small potatoes
compared to the coming good times, the lavish celebration

prepared for us. There's far more here than meets the eye. The things we see now are here today, gone tomorrow. But the things we can't see now will last forever.

For instance, we know that when these bodies of ours are taken down like tents and folded away, they will be replaced by resurrection bodies in heaven—God-made, not handmade—and we'll never have to relocate our "tents" again. Sometimes we can hardly wait to move—and so we cry out in frustration. Compared to what's coming, living conditions around here seem like a stopover in an unfurnished shack, and we're tired of it! We've been given a glimpse of the real thing, our true home, our resurrection bodies! The Spirit of God whets our appetite by giving us a taste of what's ahead. He puts a little of heaven in our hearts so that we'll never settle for less. (2 Cor. 4:16–5:5 MSG)

So let me ask again: what are we getting our bodies ready for? Not swimsuit season. Not your honeymoon. Not a 5K or even an ultramarathon. Not your next birthday party or this coming Sunday at church. The ultimate goal isn't to get our bodies ready for the day we may give birth or the mental picture we have of ourselves in our thirties, forties, or fifties. We're not getting our bodies ready to impress anyone, surprise anyone, or get revenge. We're not getting our bodies ready for the work of mission, because 2 Peter 1:3 tells us that God has given us all we need for life and godliness. So *what* are we prepping for? What are we moving toward? What's the end goal?

We're getting our bodies ready for the same reason we're readying our souls, minds, and lives of mission. We find the answer in this passage, and the answer is: *eternity*.

In fact, adding the reminder of heaven to our current equation has the potential to jar those of us who are in Christ out of this crazy earthly spin cycle of trying to get our body "right" or "finished" or "better." Because it's a little like the way we've been trying to beat the curse all along.

## The Myth of Beating the Curse

Maybe you had an aunt or a grandmother who referred to menstruation as "the curse." I know that phrase has kind of died out. But the curse is real, and the desire to beat it is alive and well.

My friend Kelly and I were pregnant together once, and her freedom left me forever changed. Our particular friend group, the specific culture that surrounded us, was obsessed (and I mean obsessed) with natural birthing. But what could have been a really empowering conversation had unfortunately turned into a condemnation station. Suddenly, there was a hierarchy being loosely established about where and how you labored.

No one overtly discussed it or passed out charts, but you could *feel* it.

So this is what I surmised about the birthing hierarchy in my friend group: The women who birthed at home were at the top—the winners. Their inflatable birthing pools (let's be honest—they were Walmart kiddie pools) became trophies of triumph that maybe stayed out for weeks—poised for the action before birth and left looming large in the living room afterward to remind us all what she'd just done.

The gals who went to a birthing center were just below the home birthers. I could never get behind the idea of a birthing center because they make you leave so quickly, and I honestly loved a nurse fussing over me for a few days. The ice chips! The help peeing! When they hand the baby to you so you can stay in bed! God bless nurses, amen.

The gals who birthed in a hospital without an epidural came

next. In my opinion, they were the most interesting—so close to the drugs, and yet so firm in their resolution to withhold. Behind them were the gals who birthed through their vaginal canal, maybe with some medication or intervention, but doing the pushing all the same.

My friend Kelly and I were at the bottom of the barrel, because we'd had C-sections. My first was an emergency C-section, but the rest were . . . (shudder) . . . planned and scheduled C-sections. I'd set a date on the calendar with my OB (usually a date I liked and thought I could remember easily), get a good night's sleep beforehand, wash my hair and shave my legs (maybe), then walk in, lie down, get hooked up to a bunch of meds, and let them cut that baby out. I didn't *want* to have C-sections, but I took the silver lining and ran with it, you know?

Anyone who has had a C-section knows that it's actually quite barbaric if you're awake, and the recovery is ridiculous because your body is healing from major surgery while you're caring for an infant who doesn't know you've been sliced in two. But if you haven't had a C-section, you may imagine it as the easy way out. And you may have been part of a community with a birthing hierarchy like we were.

Anyway, Kelly eventually had enough of it. In some ways, when the conversation shifted to birth, the two of us could sit back and relax, knowing we were removed from all the fuss. But it also made us that much more compassionate for our sisters who were putting all this pressure on one another. Here, this beautiful gift and privilege of bringing new life into the world was being reduced to a competition, being made into another realm for comparing ourselves to one another. Finally, my friend reached her limit and was ready to speak.

"Stop. Trying. To. Beat. The. Curse. Stop trying to beat the curse."

We were in somebody's kitchen during a group gathering. She said it to no one and everyone at the same time. At first it was a resolved whisper, but her voice grew louder with resolve. "Stop trying to beat the curse," she said again, and then left the room.

She was referring to Genesis 3, a passage where Eve is tricked into wanting a way out from the boundaries God has established for her. Here's what happens in that passage:

> When the Woman saw that the tree looked like good eating and realized what she would get out of it—she'd know everything!—she took and ate the fruit and then gave some to her husband, and he ate.
>
> Immediately the two of them did "see what's really going on"—saw themselves naked! They sewed fig leaves together as makeshift clothes for themselves.
>
> When they heard the sound of GOD strolling in the garden in the evening breeze, the Man and his Wife hid in the trees of the garden, hid from GOD.
>
> GOD called to the Man: "Where are you?"
>
> He said, "I heard you in the garden and I was afraid because I was naked. And I hid."
>
> GOD said, "Who told you you were naked? Did you eat from that tree I told you not to eat from?"
>
> The Man said, "The Woman you gave me as a companion, she gave me fruit from the tree, and, yes, I ate it."
>
> GOD said to the Woman, "What is this that you've done?"
>
> "The serpent seduced me," she said, "and I ate." (Gen. 3: 6–13 MSG)

It's helpful for us to pause here and note that where shame lives, blame often follows. When we feel indicted or even open to evaluation, our immediate inclination is to grab someone else and drag them under the bus with us. Adam blames Eve; Eve points out the serpent. Shame turned into blame shows up in all our cultural hierarchies because we like having some higher ground from others, but thank goodness, God deals with us individually. Let's get back to Eve and see how He deals with her.

GOD told the serpent:

> "Because you've done this, you're cursed,
>> cursed beyond all cattle and wild animals,
> cursed to slink on your belly
>> and eat dirt all your life.
> I'm declaring war between you and the Woman,
>> between your offspring and hers.
> He'll wound your head,
>> you'll wound his heel."

He told the Woman,

> "I'll multiply your pains in childbirth;
>> you'll give birth to your babies in pain.
> You'll want to please your husband,
>> but he'll lord it over you."

He told the Man:

> "Because you listened to your wife
>> and ate from the tree
> that I commanded you not to eat from,
>> 'Don't eat from this tree,'
> The very ground is cursed because of you;
>> getting food from the ground

will be as painful as having babies is for your wife;
    you'll be working in pain all your life long.
The ground will sprout thorns and weeds,
    you'll get your food the hard way,
Planting and tilling and harvesting,
    sweating in the fields from dawn to dusk,
Until you return to that ground yourself, dead and buried;
    you started out as dirt, you'll end up dirt."
        (Gen. 3:14–19 MSG)

There was an immediate consequence for the sin Adam and Eve committed: a loss of intimacy with God and expulsion from paradise. But there was also a generational and ongoing repercussion—curses that are part of living in the fallen world.

This may sound strange , but does anyone else feel strangely comforted when you're reminded of the curses we live under here on earth? In those few sentences, I'm reminded that God's absolute best for me is not extreme hormone shifts and power struggles with my husband, and that one day, those things won't be my reality. I take a deep breath and somehow smile at one of the heaviest moments in human history. The curse reminds us that life is hard because *it's not supposed to be this way.* It reminds us that the struggle is real and we're not alone in it.

But it's good to remember it's kind of crazy to try to beat the curse, amen?

Am I saying you shouldn't read birthing books or go for an empowered birthing experience? No way, sister. Read the books and buy the baby pool and get the doula, if that brings you life! But remember—it isn't a performance, and you've got nothing to prove. Giving birth is a hard experience, holy and beautiful, and there is no beating it or winning at it. There is, however, worshipping through it, like all other forms of holy work we've been invited to by God.

If it's worshipful for you to give birth with an IV in your hand or alone in a field or surrounded by friends or in a hospital or in a yurt, you do you. But while you're doing whatever you do, remember that it's a moment to experience the presence of God in your weakness, not a moment to prove how strong you are on your own. You can be comforted and surprised by His power, even His power *in* you, if you're not trying to beat the curse and prove something.

And now, back to our everyday, non-birthing bodies.

The temptation to try to beat the curse is there for all of us. For most of us, it's about forgetting the end goal and forgetting that true restoration and healing have been offered to us—on the other side of eternity. So I'd love to lead us in an exploration, an examination, of how we do this in our daily lives, how we perpetuate the quest for a better body here on this earth, forgetting that our bodies won't be made perfect until we're living in eternity.

Do you have an end goal/future self/final version of your body that you picture and work toward? Do you fight aging and illness as if your life depends on it, or as if it's completely up to you to keep your body young and well? Is there a past version of your body that you hold onto as good, rather than allowing your body to evolve and shift?

I know women who take vitamins, watch what they eat, move their bodies, and use potions and lotions on their skin as an attempt to honor the good God who made their bodies, to steward what they've been given. And I know women, including myself, who would say sometimes the exercise and eating and products and general provoking of our bodies is more about trying to hold this thing together as if it's all on us to do so, to make it good, instead of treating it as if it already is.

It's such a subtle heart difference that our only option is to check in with our motives and mindset and ask, *When it comes to how I treat my body, am I trying to beat the curse? Am I trying to outrun the effects of the fallen world?* And maybe the most beautiful question we can ask is this: *If I'm trying to beat the curse, am I missing out on the true hope and promise of restoration that heaven will bring?*

If by grace through faith you walk with God, eternity can't be taken from you. The promise that pain will go away and all will be restored is yours for the keeping, and no behavior or attitude or mistaken motivation can rob you of that healing. Here's what Revelation 21:4 says about eternity:

> He will wipe every tear from their eyes. There will be no
> more death or mourning or crying or pain, for the old order
> of things has passed away.

If you live like you can beat the curse now, you don't trade the healing that is headed your way. But you *do* miss out on the hope, and even maybe some of the comfort, that is ours to access here on earth as we feel the brokenness of this world and wait for the one to come. I imagine that living as though you can beat the curse would lead to frustration with yourself, the space around you, and even God, as well as less delight in His comfort both here and in eternity.

We can pluck, pull, squat, detox, wear the Spanx, drink the water, take the vitamins, use the supplements, slather on the potions, do the yoga, and wash our faces to our hearts' content. But hear me: As long as you remain convinced that your body is your responsibility alone to "fix," your heart will not be content. And your body will not stop experiencing brokenness. Not until eternity. Not until the curse is broken in full by the only One who has the power to break it, and you experience the resurrection of your body that was purchased with His. So we must care for our bodies with eternity in mind, and in the meantime take comfort that we don't serve a God who asked us to heal ourselves. He has a good plan that cannot be thwarted, and we can rest in it as we worship and steward these bodies on earth.

## Rest in the Land

Gravity, pollution, sickness, illness, time, age, work, stress, pain, and even joy are altering our bodies daily. This is the curse of a fallen world at work, right? Our bodies are groaning under the weight of being human, and there's a fine line between taking care of them as best we can while we're here and trying to beat the curse that leaves us susceptible to weakness in our flesh.

For many of us, I believe one of the most cunning and confusing proposals we're given is, "If you did _____ to your body, then _____ would happen."

We've been taught by our culture to ignore the fact that our bodies are the intentional creations of a good and loving Father, not an unstable measurement of how good or worthy we are. Our bodies were made and called good, we were made and called good, and the work of our lives is not to spend the rest of our time making them acceptable or able to measure up to whatever standard the culture has established for bodies right now.

For each one of us, it begins at a different age and with varying levels of heartbreak, but we're told a lie that we can beat the curse of living in these aging and decaying bodies by improving them, and thus, improving ourselves. The truth is, we're all preparing for heaven, which will be the most real and wonderful part of our existence; our bodies were made good by an intentional Father, and they're suffering the effects of being here on this earth, groaning and longing for relief. Our bodies can be healed, our bodies can grow stronger, and we can become more in tune with God, right here in our bodies. But first, we have to break ties with this idea that they have to become better according to the standard of the world in order to be counted as worthy.

We must get quiet and ask ourelves: *What is my body for? Why has God given it to me? Is it good already, or is the goal to be making it better? How do I take care of it, experience it, and feel about it?*

If you sit with these questions long enough, my hunch is that, like me, you'll experience an increasing sense of weariness, because that's what comes from trying to beat an unbeatable curse. It's exhausting to spend all our energy fighting a battle that isn't ours to win.

A few years ago, I got wildly excited about the story of Moses and Joshua and the promise of the land to which God would lead the Israelites. Moses' story is one of bravery and doubt, faithfulness and holding back, worship and struggling with the approval of the people he was leading—often all at once. As a consequence of his sin, when it's time for his people to enter the promised land, he's only allowed to see it—not to enter in with them. He dies, and God appoints and commissions Joshua to take his place as leader.

But at the very beginning, in the section of Scripture labeled, "The Taking of the Land," Joshua reminds his people of some specific words from God:

> Then Joshua gave orders to the people's leaders: "Go through the camp and give this order to the people: 'Pack your bags. In three days you will cross this Jordan River to enter and take the land GOD, your God, is giving you to possess.'"
>
> Then Joshua addressed the Reubenites, the Gadites, and the half-tribe of Manasseh. He said, "Remember what Moses

the servant of GOD commanded you: God, **your God, gives you rest and he gives you this land.** Your wives, your children, and your livestock can stay here east of the Jordan, the country Moses gave you; but you, tough soldiers all, must cross the River in battle formation, leading your brothers, helping them until GOD, your God, gives your brothers a place of rest just as he has done for you. They also will take possession of the land that GOD, your God, is giving them. Then you will be free to return to your possession, given to you by Moses the servant of GOD, across the Jordan to the east." (Joshua 1:10–15 MSG, emphasis mine)

I was thinking that day about the land God gives each of us, individually, for rest. I believe His promise of rest is not just for the Israelites. Psalm 127:2 says He gives rest to those He loves. And I know He loves me! So in this world of toil and turmoil, what is my soft place to land? Where can I be at ease in the love and favor and goodness of God?

*What if that vessel, that space, was the very body He created good and holy just for me? What if this body is the land He's given me to inherit, to experience more of Him in?*

What if I've taken what was meant to be a gift and treated it as a project, as an ever-changing monitor of my goodness and worth, as a trophy declaring that I've beaten the curse of aging and of living in a place where everything decays? What if I've taken this good gift, exhausted it and examined it, and forgotten that it is supposed to be a safe space where God allows me to experience His presence and power here on earth? For many of us, it wasn't a conscious choice, but a path we were placed on and have been following ever since. I don't think it's too late for us to go back. I don't think it's too late for us to experience rest in our land.

It seems that God loves giving rest to people in the place where they belong. Don't we believe that God wants rest for us as we come home to our bodies—the setting where He has intentionally and uniquely placed us? Surely it's not His desire for us to continue living in shame as it pertains to the holy space of our skin. When we *come home* to our bodies, the place where God has uniquely created us to belong, we can experience rest, too. When we embrace that we belong here, in *this* good body, we can experience rest.

## Rest for the Land

If I asked you what life was like in March 2019, you may not be able to remember. But I assume most of us will always be able to recall what life was like in March 2020. And April 2020. And the whole summer of 2020—which is the season I currently am writing in. A pandemic has hit not only the United States, but the entire world. The days are a rollercoaster of fear and confusion, gratitude and grace—almost everyone I know knows someone who has gotten sick and or died. Almost everyone I know is also trying to somehow make the most of each day and find the silver lining in this debilitating and confusing time.

But something happened to the earth during the pandemic. They say the land began to heal. Some of the harmful effects of globalization were reversing with just a few months of humans traveling less. I didn't know ocean noise (the sounds made by human activities that can interfere with or obscure the ability of marine animals to hear natural sounds in the ocean) was a problem until I found out recently that the early months of the pandemic has caused its reversal as well to some degree. The whales and dolphins and various sea creatures are now more at peace because the huge boats and cruise ships are docked for the time being. People around the world are saying the birds seem louder, which I can attest to myself—but it's only because our noise pollution is down significantly. The earth will go back to "normal," meaning more damaged, once we begin traveling and moving again.[1]

This has caused me to wonder what kind of healing, what kind of radical change is possible if we rest our bodies in the same way, if we put a hard stop on the noise, the constant motion, the bustle and busyness.

During those first months of the pandemic, I noticed my body groaning more and healing at the same time. I noticed some rest in my land. I've never been more aware of what's happening in my flesh—without so much to distract me. At first I noticed my anxiety, inhabiting so many different functions in my body. The fear was escaping my pores through sweat, my hands through a slight tremor, my face through the effects of hormones. I tried not to be angry, just to notice the pain coming to the surface.

I noticed how much sorer I was as my movement varied and shifted. I wasn't going from place to place to place any longer. I stayed at home and moved in spurts. Long walks in the morning, sitting or only moving so much during the day, exercising in the afternoon, and one more long walk with the kids before bed.

As the initial panic wore off, I began sleeping more than I have in fifteen years. I noticed what it was like when I didn't yawn through the afternoon or need more than one or two cups of coffee. My husband's ongoing, years-long battle with tension neck pain all but disappeared after a few weeks of being home. As the hurry and striving ceased because there was no other option, many of the physiological symptoms we had learned to live with disappeared. In some ways, the land was getting rest. In

---

1. "Seas Quieted by Pandemic Could Reduce Stress," *National Geographic*, July 2020, https://www.nationalgeographic.com/science/2020/07/seas -silenced-by-pandemic-could-improve-health-whales/?awc=19533_1602939703 _e3c47dac75dd2e79fb9309a48d4d7d91.

other ways, the land and our collective bodies have experienced trauma and stress that's almost indescribable.

Five months into the pandemic hitting the US, despite being incredibly cautious for months, my entire family contracted COVID-19. The experience of what happened in my body, even beyond the symptoms of the virus, was wild. I will never forget it as long as I live. I'll never forget the nights I had honest and humble conversations with God as I struggled to get one of my kids' temperature down. As a mother, I felt fragile, hopeful, and still somewhat helpless—more tangibly aware of my need for God and His healing than I had in the past. I'll never forget filling my lungs with air over and over again, measuring just how well I could breathe with gratitude and fear combined in each inhale. I'll never forget how incredibly aware I was of my capacity to speak life over my own body and the bodies of my loved ones, while also feeling so distinctly submitted to the mercy and kindness of God.

When it was all said and done, our symptoms were mild, and we all recovered completely and quickly. But even the mildness of our experience pushed me to trust God in entirely new ways.

At the end of the day, I was left grateful for the body He'd given me, but so much more grateful for His grace and the promise of eternity than I'd ever been.

What's wild is that I experienced new levels of rest when I wasn't sick and new levels of rest when I was. The healing, the hope of being off the hook from striving and holding all things together, is available to us when the setting is seemingly right *and* when it's not. Your body gets to be at rest, whether you are your ideal size and level of wellness or not. God gives rest to those He loves, not to those who have earned it as a reward.

Many of us may want to read this book and others like it because we want our bodies to be better. We know that there is a connection between our mind, our hearts, and our bodies—and somewhere, deep in our souls, we hope that if we think or feel or know the right things, our bodies will begin to improve. This is where I tell you vulnerably that the enemy of my own soul has tempted me with the same provocation: *Maybe if you write this book, you'll finally get your junk together and get your body right.*

But I perceive that more than we need our bodies to get *better*, we need to rest in the unshakeable truth that they were made *good*. And part of agreeing with that eternal truth is learning to rest in the land and allowing it to get some rest.

Just as our land experienced some rest during the pandemic, when we stopped provoking it with copious travel, I perceive that many of us won't experience true rest until we stop provoking our bodies with strategies and tactics aimed at making it "better." Until we come home to our bodies, appreciating the way they were made good by God, we will continue to misunderstand our responsibility to our bodies. We'll provoke our bodies.

What if we completely removed the performative if/then statements we make about our bodies? What if we made a collective decision that we would only treat our bodies in accordance with what God has said about them? What if we decided that we couldn't beat the curse of being human for now, but we can look forward to the moment when we experience the true form we were meant to take in heaven? What if we lived and treated our bodies not in accordance with earning the approval of man in mind, but with eternity in mind? What if we looked at our flesh and said, "You owe me nothing, but I will treat you with honor and kindness because you were made by God and called good"?

## Invisible Wheelchairs and Broken Thyroids

This is a perfect place to pause and address those of us who have very real grief regarding the fallen state of our bodies. Maybe you identify with my friend Katherine, who experienced a horrific stroke, or my friend Heather, who has battled infertility. My friend Taylor was shot in a school shooting and lives with debilitating pain because of it. My friend Gabby has fibromyalgia, and I've watched her weep through the pain after leading our church in worship. For many of us, the grief isn't that we don't look the way we want to in a bathing suit—the grief is that we live with chronic pain or fatigue or frustration or feeling limited in ways others do not.

In so many ways, these friends of mine teach me how to have compassion for my flesh as they live expectantly for heaven. They call me to a new level of learning to love my body because God made it, even when I'm deeply disappointed by and frustrated with it.

When I was first beginning to wrestle with my own autoimmune disease diagnosis years and years ago, I posted something on social media about being mad at my thyroid. As hilarious and immature as it was, I believe I said something to the effect of, "If I could punch my thyroid, I would." I'll never forget the comment of an older and wiser friend, who responded with something along the lines of, "No! Your thyroid is your body—you should love it and treat it kindly." I remember being frustrated, feeling like she had dismissed my pain and agitation. I remember thinking that if she had a thyroid that was giving her as many issues as mine was giving me, she'd be angry, too.

My friend Katherine, who lives her life in a wheelchair, says we all live in invisible wheelchairs. We've all got some suffering or some handicap, even if we can't see it. But I've noticed that my friends with visible handicaps or injuries, the ones who've been in a traumatic fight alongside their bodies instead of against them, seem to have a feeling of gratitude toward their own flesh that is so encouraging. It's like they can look at their ailing thyroid and say, "Hey—what's not working for you right now? What's the problem?" instead of, "You are a real pain in the neck (that's a joke, because your thyroid is in your neck), and I hate you. I wish I could punch you."

I think about the thyroid comment even now—twelve years later. Which of us was right? Is it OK or even productive to be angry at your body when it doesn't have a separate soul or will? Would gentleness and kindness be a more helpful tool in the healing process? What does it even mean to be angry at your body when your body is *you*? What if many of us who experience bitterness toward our bodies actually have pain we need to process with our souls and with our Savior?

I want to officially welcome any of you who have visible "wheelchairs," as Katherine would say, even if you don't have literal wheelchairs. I've learned that safe spaces are less realistic to expect, but brave spaces can be built, and I pray this book is that for you. I pray you hear the same message as everyone else, and with emphatic encouragement: *Your body is good.* I pray our culture would consider the constraints of your body more and more daily as we repent from the ideals we strive for and confess our own blindness, our inability to see the burdens of others. I pray this message is a brave space where you feel considered, championed, and invited to lead the conversation. Thank you for being here.

## Your Invitation to Rest

The invitation to rest from striving and the eternal attempt to get better gives these bodies of flesh a moment to escape our critiquing and contending and comparing. The invitation to rest gives our hearts and minds a moment to ask and answer important questions about what our bodies are for in the first place, rather than continuing on in the assumptions we've lived under in an automatic way. The invitation to rest creates a pause where we can ask: who am I actually mad at or frustrated with? Who am I actually disappointed by? And how can I direct those feelings in a way that is potentially more fruitful and less harmful to my own body?

I'm going to invite you into a few new practices in this book, some of which you may have already picked up on. Some will take time to establish, some you'll pick up on immediately and automatically, and some you may wrestle with the rest of your life. I've already invited you to slow down and consider how we got here—to listen to the messages you've received about your body, to dive back into potentially painful memories that have shaped your perception of your own flesh. I've asked you to pay attention to the naming power of God, to your own naming power, and the naming power other people have had in your life. I've invited you to stop speaking death over your own body, and instead, to consider what God would say about His creation, made with love and intention.

And now, I'm going to invite you to *consider* resting the land. What if you gave yourself the space and time—maybe, say, the time it would take to read this book—to stop striving and seeing if your body *can* be made better. What if you looked at yourself literally and metaphorically and said, "You don't have to be improving right now. You are good as you are"? What if instead of letting your feelings of frustration, disappointment, and defeat crash in like daily waves, you noticed those feelings and tried to redirect them away from your body?. I'm picturing us not necessarily trying to hold back the tide from coming in, but sitting in the tension of a sea of feelings, and asking each wave, "Where did you come from, and where should you go?"

Imagine your soul standing over your body for this moment in time and saying, "You can't mess with her. She was made good. It's not her job to fit any mold, live up to any standard, or win the approval of any man. She is good. And she is resting right now."

I'd love to suggest three simple ways you can rest the land right now, beginning today and continuing on.

- Break ties with the concept of "ideal weight." Maybe it's a number you've seen before, one you were told would be right for you, or one you've been aiming at for years. Talk to God. Ask Him if it's OK to give up chasing this number, and then just capture and speak truth to any future thoughts that point back to that number as a goal.

- Identify a beauty or wellness routine that is not life-giving to you but feels like something you "should" do. Consider quitting. Allow yourself to ask why it became a routine, who you're worshipping when you engage in it, and what would happen if you quit it altogether.

- Pay attention to any rhythms of withholding and/or treating yourself. Are certain things off-limits unless you earn them with healthy behavior? What would it look like to let your body just be without stringent restrictions and/or rewards for good behavior?

I've told you already I live with a pretty frustrating autoimmune disease. I don't really have the option to stop caring for my body, so I would never advocate for that. My body needs movement and healthy food. She needs respite and renewal, and together, we're continually figuring out what helps her function best. Sometimes, I ignore what she needs for long periods and then pay the price for it. So when I ask you to rest the land, I'm not inviting you to forsake healthy living. Instead, I'm encouraging you to look at the intentions behind your activities and ask, *Am I doing this to love her or to make her into something I can love?*

My commitment is that I'll do the same, even though it is not the most natural default for me. I promise to rest my land as I write and as this book begins to come to the surface, to fight the enemy's lie that my body is any kind of indicator of achievement or usefulness for this message. I will rest my land and keep encouraging you to do the same because the alternative is that we will continually act as aggressive accusers, telling our own flesh how it needs to fit in.

So take a breath. You're off the hook. Your body is good because He said so. It's time for the land to get some rest.

## Questions

What are you getting your body ready for?

Would you like to pull the lever and scream "stop" too?
Would you like to stop trying to "get your body right"?

What would it look like for you to let your body rest
from the ongoing work of "making it better"?

What will your soul say for your body
when anything tries to provoke her?

# Words from Our Friends

**Tiffany:** *What if we looked at our flesh and told it, "You owe me nothing. But I will treat you with honor and kindness because you were made by God and called good.?" I'm convicted. My body has been so good to me, and I have pushed it to its limits. It has carried me through four years of college, four years of optometry school, conceived babies, carried babies, leading worship, and many dance classes and recitals. I have dragged it to playdates and soccer games, thrown parties with it, used it to decorate for friends' celebrations. I just keep going. I don't tell you about my tendency to "just keep going" in order to get applause, though. Honestly, this tendency has landed me in many specialists' offices as they try to figure out the reasons for my burning skin, racing heart, gastritis, and pain. The answer is stress. My body has been good to me, but I have not always been kind to it. Now, I'm aware when it is begging for rest. The Lord has given us rest, but I refused to accept it in the past, believing I was somehow failing if I gave in to my need to rest. But who am I to tell God I don't need what He's ordained? What am I saying about my trust in Him when I do not accept what He has offered me? He is not only sovereign. He is good, and His gift of rest is good for me.*

**Kati:** *My version of cerebral palsy is what they call spastic quadriplegic cerebral palsy, and it affects my whole body. Basically, the motor skills portion of my brain didn't form correctly because I was born prematurely. My brain tells my muscles not to function "properly." Picture a thick rubber band stretched to capacity. That is my muscles' normal state, even when resting. Now, imagine pushing on that taut rubber band. That is my muscles moving, if at all. It* takes a lot of effort and "energy points" to move, walk, stand, even sit—more effort than I ever realized until I had surgery in 2016. I pushed my body hard all my life in order to be someone I could love and someone others would (hopefully) like, but what ultimately happened was that I became something that felt successful in the eyes of the world: being a mama. While I was happy doing what I was doing (it's an amazing job!), I never felt worthy of the love and admiration of the people around me, of God, of my family, and definitely not of myself. In my eyes, my worth was still measured by what I could do for others, not simply based on who I am—and I could never do enough for the people I loved and cared about.

Now, I look back and am grateful for rest, because I see where I was and where I am now. God knew I would have a grandson to look after in this season, and I that I would need to be mobile. I have learned so much about myself and my body in these last few years, and I have also grown more in my relationship with God as He's revealed His handiwork through hindsight. It has taught me how to care for my body going forward, at least as far as mobility is concerned, and I'm grateful.

# CHAPTER 6

# Your Body Is Not a Project

My dad lived overseas when I was young, and when I was eleven or twelve, his visits home lived in the calendar of my mind as opportunities to prove myself. How would I look the next time he saw me? Would I have "thinned out," as we praise young girls for doing? Would I look healthy and put together? Would I look more mature? Or would it be yet another visit wherein Messy Jessi would show up—sloppy and soft, predictable and precious all the same?

My dad's visits were the first time I ever began viewing my body as being on a timeline: Will it be better? Will it be enough? Will it be OK?

It wasn't my dad's fault. He didn't say anything to provoke my project-based body thoughts. He wasn't the enemy. The enemy was the evil force that wages war against my soul. The enemy was cultural expectations, the picture-perfect idea of what a daughter and father should look like at varying stages of their relationship. The enemy was the way I used time to torment and cause trauma to my body, counting occasions and celebrations as deadlines and due dates.

Eventually, my dad moved home again, but the questions remained, simmering beneath the surface for years. The morning I left for college, loading up all my belongings in my car, my boyfriend's car, and my parents' car, happened to be my eighteenth birthday. So much independence and so many milestones in one day! We heaved laundry baskets into the back seats and arranged boxes in our vehicles while the South Carolina summer air caused sweat to pool on our backs, even though it was early in the day. Nick drove behind me and my parents behind him, while I went in my own car—appreciating the two-hour drive as an opportunity to be alone with my thoughts on such an important day.

I watched my arm resting against the car window, my skin spreading slightly on the glass, and I thought, *Something's not right. I'm not supposed to look like this.* I'd always pictured myself going to college and looking smaller, more mature, more put together, less like . . . me. Reality wasn't lining up with the vision I'd carried of who I would be by now. The project had not been completed, at least not well. My stomach fluttered, and I flashed back to December 1995, the first time I stood at the airport waiting for my dad and feeling like I hadn't done enough, like *I* wasn't enough. I realized the thoughts I was having now at eighteen echoed the thoughts that came rushing in when I stood at the bottom of the escalator at the airport, waiting for my dad to descend. *Was I OK? Did I measure up? Was I what he expected? Was I what I expected?*

I drove on. There was no one to answer my questions. Over

time, the questions turned into resolutions, promises to always have the "project" completed by due date after due date.

> My wedding day
> The day I started my first real job
> The first time I taught the Bible
> A mission trip
> Every birthday
> Other people's birthdays
> Book launches
> Vacations
> Anniversaries

I treated my body like a project for months before my wedding, eating as little as possible and moving as much as possible. Before my first day at my very first job, I practiced doing my hair over and over again, determined to make sure I looked mature and fashionable from every angle. Preparing to teach the Bible for the first time, I meditated over ways I could make my body look better more than I meditated on the Word of God. Every birthday became less about marking what God had done in my life that year and more about prepping my body to look good in pictures. Every sacred moment was invaded by the sense, like a ticking time bomb, that I only had so many days, hours, workouts, and meals to get ready . . . but for what? For just another second of self-evaluation in the never-ending project that was living in my body. With every such evaluation, I made room for defeat, shame, pride, and failure to have too much say.

Most major events in my life came attached with a prefixed perception of what I would like when the day arrived. Sometimes I pictured myself as svelte, but for the most part, if I'm honest, I wasn't necessarily craving to be smaller. I just wanted to look *put together*. I wanted to look tidy. I wanted to look ready and prepared for the moment. I wanted to look like I belonged. Something rooted deep in my heart was telling me I wasn't any of those things.

In the months leading up to my wedding, I didn't feel ready to get married. I was worried I was too young—the same way everyone else worried I was too young. I didn't know if I could sustain a marriage; I didn't know if I could make it work. I didn't feel responsible or devoted or even slightly mature enough to love a man and build a life.

If I could go back now and gently coach or encourage the twenty-year-old Jess, who walked down the aisle more focused on her non-existent back fat than on the fears bubbling up inside her, I'd ask her how she was feeling, and then I'd ask again. I'd tell her that not *feeling* ready wasn't an indicator of not *being* ready. I'd tell her she was right to tremble at the idea of committing to life with another soul, but it didn't mean he wasn't the right soul.

I'd tell her it will be terrifying, but God will be there and give her grace for each day. I'd tell her she doesn't have to walk down the aisle with the wisdom of a wife, she just gets to boldly make promises she can't keep because that is the nature of a bride. Grace does the rest. Because I know this much exhortation would probably freak her out, I'd also offer her the opportunity to run, but I'd warn her that if she does, she'll miss out on spending her life with the most gracious, most patient man she'll ever meet. I wouldn't tell her about the four kids and the dog and the church and the cross-country moves they'll make, but I would tell her Jesus loves them both individually, and will love their marriage with the fierce devotion that she didn't feel she had.

And I wonder if, rather than berating her for thinking about her body, speaking to her soul would help her shift her focus. I wonder if reminding her of the power that is present in the midst of her weakness would help her feel less like a project that needs to be completed before some ominous due date. I wonder if feeling spiritually and emotionally healthy could have helped her do a better job of caring for her physical body in the midst of that moment.

When you think of your body as a project with a deadline, what comes to mind? Maybe for you it's vacations—or, scratch that, it's the entire vacation *season*, otherwise known as the "summer body," the ultimate "body as project" mentality. How many of us have treated our bodies as projects to be completed by the start of summer?

Some things we pick up from no one in particular, while others we pick up from our culture, which is screaming a message that cannot possibly be ignored. This is the story of the summer body and our elusive search for it.

You start hearing it in workout classes in January. It's on TV and the radio by March. Depending on your life season, your friends, coworkers, and family members may discuss it around lunch tables or on walks or during catch-up phone calls. The start of summer body looms, and the first presentation of the project is due. I grew up hating summer with a passion because everyone seemed to be on the same page about what it meant to be "ready" for it, and I couldn't ever quite get there.

Lovingly, can I ask if we can get on another page? All of us? This page is horrible. Let's break down why it's the pits. I'll be focusing mainly on how we treat women's bodies as projects, but I know this is an issue that plagues men, too. What happens when we choose to treat our bodies as projects? At least three things, none of them good.

1. *When we treat our bodies as projects, we agree with the enemy—however unconsciously—that women are mere objects.* When we begin to dip our toes into the swirling and perilous

waters of "getting our bodies ready for summer," it's important to be aware that a dark, formidable, and evil movement of the enemy underlies this normalized conversation.

Let's make no mistake about it: the enemy of our souls is on a mission to cause pain and wreak havoc through the objectification of women's bodies. From sexual assault to the modern-day sex slave trade to the brutalization of women's bodies in developing countries to the pandemic-sized problem of pornography, the enemy is attacking the world using the objectification of women's bodies as a vehicle.

It's as if, somewhere along the way, the idea popped into his head—"I can just treat them as things. Detach them from their souls, their minds, their roles in the kingdom. I can get men to treat their bodies like objects to be used and abused. That will mess *everyone* up."

I want to pause here and tell you I know that, for many of us, these words aren't empty. They're attached to painful memories, traumatic experiences, true moments that we'd give everything we've got to have missed. I want to invite us all to ask God to show us where He was when our respective traumas occurred, where His heart was in the midst of the pain. Where is He now, when so many women's bodies are still not safe? Let's take a look at God's answer to this essential question:

> But now, GOD's Message,
> > the God who made you in the first place, Jacob,
> > the One who got you started, Israel:
> "Don't be afraid, I've redeemed you.
> > I've called your name. You're mine.
> When you're in over your head, I'll be there with you.
> > When you're in rough waters, you will not go down.
> When you're between a rock and a hard place,

it won't be a dead end—
Because I am God, your personal God,
    The Holy of Israel, your Savior.
I paid a huge price for you:
    all of Egypt, with rich Cush and Seba thrown in!
*That's* how much you mean to me!
    *That's* how much I love you!
I'd sell off the whole world to get you back,
    trade the creation just for you. (Isaiah 43:1–4 MSG)

The Lord is close to the brokenhearted
    and saves those who are crushed in spirit. (Psalm 34:18)

He heals the brokenhearted
    and binds up their wounds. (Psalm 147:3)

Our Father created women with intention and care, and He treasures their bodies as well as their souls. He made us with the vision of more than just earthly existence in mind—He made us with eternal worth, impact, and vision.

Our Father grieves the falling more than we ever could. He would not have chosen for us to live in brokenness and bondage. In love, he provided a rescue through His Son. Our Father binds us up when we're broken-hearted, calls our crushed spirits closer to His, holds us and brings healing like time and other people never can.

What does all this have to do with getting our bodies ready for summer? In a small way, a way in which we may not have even known that we're partnering with the enemy, when we feel the need to get our bodies ready for any season or event, we're agreeing that women's bodies aren't worthy of being treated like souls but of being treated like objects.

This is one area of our lives where we can draw a firm boundary and say, *I will not agree with the enemy. I will not allow my body to be treated like an object. I will not even dip a toe into the dark, teeming waters of objectifying women and separating their worth from their souls for a moment.*

2. *When we treat our bodies as projects, we shift the focus from God's glory to our own.* For many of us, our root desire or motivation in treating our bodies like projects isn't objectification. We may not have known we were partnering with the enemy in his attack because objectification isn't what's in our own hearts. What may very well be in our hearts, though, is a desire for our own glory, or more specifically, a desire for our bodies to be praised by others.

One of the enemy's most cunning and effective strategies is to corrupt our focus. In an attempt to value women's bodies, we've confused celebration and glorification. We've confused giving God glory for something good He's made and craving glory for our own bodies, which ultimately detracts the focus from our good God.

> I am the LORD; that is my name!
>     I will not yield my glory to another
>     or my praise to idols. (Isaiah 42:8)

I'll start (and stay) with myself since this is a tension-filled topic. If I'm honest, I have a desire planted not so deeply in my heart for others to praise me. Even as a kid, I craved attention and approval. As a child, I didn't know better, but as an adult, I *do*. Now, as a follower of Jesus who seeks to give and bring Him glory, I can work from a place of conviction and honesty to confess that when I treat my body like a project, part of what I'm picturing when the project is "completed" is the glory and praise others will give my body.

This desire is both sinful and not what I was made for. I was made to bring *God* glory. When I find myself wanting God's glory for myself, it's essentially idol worship of the creation He made to *give* Himself glory.

There's a distinction between celebrating what God has created and worshipping the created thing itself. Do we celebrate the families God has given us or worship them? Do we celebrate the church as the family of God or give it undue praise? Do we give God glory as we consume the food He's given us or make it an idol our lives revolve around?

Answering these questions takes discernment, listening to the Spirit of God, and being honest about what's in our hearts. To ask these questions—to allow God to ask these questions of us—takes bravery and a belief in the righteousness of Christ. But the questions are worth asking.

If we are able to draw a direct line between treating our bodies like projects and craving praise and glory, we can and should repent of and stop partnering with that practice immediately. Amen?

3. *When we treat our bodies as projects, we miss out on the abundance God already has for us in our here-and-now lives.* Our church talks a lot about abundance. My family talks a lot about abundance. I write a good bit about abundance. I love the idea of abundance.

> "The thief comes only to steal and kill and destroy; I have come that they may have life, and have it to the full." (John 10:10)

The phrase "to the full" in Greek is περισσός, or *perissos*, and it means *abundant*. Specifically, it means more, greater, in excess, beyond what is anticipated, going past the expected limit.

If we read the Bible in snippets and pockets, without looking at the broad context of what God values and teaches throughout all of Scripture, we could be tempted to interpret "abundance" to mean more of what the earth values. We might believe that abundance means more comfort, more money, more stuff. As a whole, Scripture helps us remember that the things of this world will fade and burn (1 Cor. 7:31), that wealth can actually be a stumbling stone when it comes to understanding the kingdom (Matt. 19:24), and following Jesus often requires a breaking of allegiance to our stuff (Matt. 19:21).

In light of this, we've got to remember that the "more," the abundance that Jesus came to bring us, is spiritual and thus, eternal. It's peace. It's comfort. It's His presence. It's His power! It's renewal. It's vision. It's healing. It's hope! It's mission and purpose and passion that is ours for the taking. It's all this and more—it's abundance, purchased for us on the cross of Christ.

And what if we're missing out on this abundance right now because we're stuck in a project-based mentality about our bodies? What if we're believing we have to achieve or earn abundance by making ourselves look more like our culture expects us to? What if we've misunderstood the concept of abundance entirely because we've bought the lie that the best thing we can have is a "good body" when we already have good bodies?

What if the enemy couldn't take us out or take our gifts or wreck our lives, so He just made us wish we could be better from an earthly standpoint? What if we're missing out on the true, eternal, spiritual understanding of seasons and what God does in and through them because we're trying to get "summer bodies" and treating our flesh as if it's a project to be completed?

Can we treat our bodies like the good gifts they are? Can we declare them good, just as they are right now, and remember that the most important thing we bring to the table is our souls?

## The Truest Thing about You

It's time to introduce another hero in my personal body story. Her name is Meredith. She's my counselor, and I could spend the rest of this chapter telling you amazing and hilarious stories about her. The amazing stories center around the wisdom and insight she provides without fail. She's tough and tender, and genuinely one of the best women I know.

The funny stories? Those are about my unprofessional attachment to Meredith. Once, when I ran into her at a coffee shop, I wasn't sure if it would be breaking some sort of code if I said hello. I did eventually say "Hi," but then I also unfortunately ended up telling her I loved her, too. Then I had to tell her I was sorry I had said I loved her, but that I did indeed love her. That about sums things up.

Meredith has been a hero in my journey to believing my body is good. I'm incredibly grateful for her. Once, I was preparing my heart and processing my personal fears about being a bridesmaid in a dear friend's wedding. I love my friend and couldn't wait to stand beside her, but I was feeling pretty insecure about my body. I described to Meredith all the characteristics of the situation that concerned me (wearing a dress that didn't fit my body style, standing in front of people and feeling seen, and having my picture taken so many times) when she asked me the golden question:

"What is the truest thing about you? What do you bring into every one of these spaces that you enter?"

I'm pretty sure I had to leave our session that day without answering because I had to think about it. There were a lot of answers I wanted to give, but they felt like what I was supposed to say and not what I knew to be true.

It took me a few weeks, but I got to my answer, and the truth of it is still transforming me.

The truest thing about me, the most valuable aspect of myself that I bring into every situation and relationship is that God loves me, calls me His friend, and has made me His ambassador.

This truth doesn't rely on *my* work or *my* goodness, so it doesn't become false after a hard day or in a tough season. But the fact that I'm loved transforms how I love and serve others. It compels me to give all I have and take what I need. It shifts me and sends me. It changes my perspective in the moment and pushes me out into the future with a purpose. The fact that God has called me a friend is what *makes* me able to be a friend to others. The calling, mission, vision, and purpose He has written into my life enables me to walk through the world with hope and healing in my hands.

Being loved, cared for, and sent by God is what helps me walk into any wedding full of light and love, and that is more transforming than how I look in any bridesmaid's dress.

The same is true of you, my friend. We can reject the notion that our bodies are projects to keep tinkering with because that notion is rooted in the dark and demonic objectification of women. We can run from the temptation to continually provoke our bodies and obsess about getting them "right," because they were made good to begin with, and we don't want to set our hearts on stealing glory from God by trying to seek it for ourselves. We can reject any notion that suggests that our bodies are the most important or notable parts of us, because we know that our souls also carry beauty and worth into the world.

We are not projects. We are daughters of God, bought at a price, given gifts and skills and callings that can literally change the world. We're not hoping to be remembered by the size of our thighs or the shine of our hair or our ability to "bounce back" after having a baby. We're here to shine the light of Jesus, to love our neighbors, to use what we've got for the good of others and the glory of God. We are not projects; we are ambassadors, and we're not going to be tricked again into believing anything else. Amen?

## Put It into Practice

Let's keep our rhythm of not just retaining knowledge, but putting truth into action.

**First, some hard questions:**

1. *When and how are you most tempted to treat your body like a project?*

   Is it summer? Vacations? When you're going to see certain friends? If I'm honest, the times I'm most tempted to treat my body like a project or a test on which I'll be scored are the times I'm called to use my spiritual gifts. Important Sundays at church, the days my kids get baptized, book launches, even significant celebrations that are about other people. This discourages me greatly because I know the energy that goes into worrying about my body and "preparing" it would be so much better spent preparing my heart. I know the enemy has won some ground in these moments, as I've made them about me and not about the kingdom of God, and that grieves me.

2. *How can you actively stop agreeing that women's bodies are open for objectification in your life?*

   I pray the Holy Spirit is gentle and complete in guiding us to honesty as we ask ourselves this question.

3. *Where and how can you seek to give God glory with your body?*

   I'm a big fan of replacement as a tool of repentance. If you've been spending a substantial amount of time and energy seeking your own glory through your body, how can you use that energy to give God glory with your body? How can you lead? Serve? Speak about His truth? Can you go on a worship walk? Have a praise dance party? What could this look like for you?

4. *What's the truest thing about you?*

## Now, let's try some life-giving practices:

1. *Practice being present in your body and in your life this week.* What's going well? What good things need your attention and your gratitude? What hard things need your attention and your prayer?

   I can never quite get over how spending quiet time with myself and my God reframes the way I see my body *and* the way I treat my body. For ten minutes or two hours, practice being present in your body.

2. *Go to God to replace the "project" with prayer.* Again, I think replacement is a big part of renewing our minds. We can't just hope we'll change; we often have to put something positive where something negative has resided.

3. *Ask God to give you vision for something bigger than yourself that does not involve making your body acceptable to the culture.* Ask Him for a calling, a task, or a prayer to which you can devote your energy.

4. *Go back to an important moment from your past, when you treated your body like a project.* Ask God for eyes to see it the way He did. Ask Him for the ability to notice where He was and how ready you were, regardless of how your body looked.

# Words from Our Friends

**Ariana:** *I'm so glad Jess has called out the enemy's mission to objectify women's bodies. And I want to acknowledge that his mission manifests in ways that are sometimes specific to our cultures and body types.*

*I didn't grow up wanting the version of beauty the media sold. I am Puerto Rican, so my goals were a little different (hello, JLo!). A thick, hourglass figure is the norm in my family. So I was happy to mature into a young woman after being a super-skinny, "flat" girl in my early years.*

*That joy didn't last long, though. My body attracted a lot of unwanted attention. I was harassed by boys more aggressively than other girls. I was told I would have to wear baggier clothing if I wanted to sing on the worship team. I learned that my body, the one I had been so grateful to get, was seen by the world as a stumbling block no matter how modest I tried to be. Instead of joy or pride, I wore shame and walked in fear of corrupting men by just wearing a pair of jeans.*

*Ladies, shame is not for us. Let's come out of agreement with the enemy's mission against our bodies.*

*Repeat after me: My body is not a table set for sin.*

CHAPTER 7

# Restoring Your Body to Its Original Purpose

*I will restore you to health*
*and heal your wounds,*
*declares the LORD. (Jer. 30:17)*

Confession: I am an obnoxious question asker, and I can't stop it. As a kid, I'd ask really probing questions, often at inopportune times, because why not? My mom used to call them "Jessi-isms." All throughout my childhood, she'd joke that she was writing them down, collecting them to someday put in a book. Looking back, I don't think it was curiosity that drove my questions but confusion over things that were considered the status quo. If something was generally accepted by others but didn't make sense to me, I'd say so, even if it wasn't culturally appropriate to do so. The silliest one we both remember is that there was a big hill in our neighborhood. On the side where you drove up, there was a traffic sign that read, "HILL." One day I told my mom how dumb that seemed to me—why have a sign that stated the obvious?

I wasn't obsessed with *how* things were but with *why* they were. I never tried to take apart a DVD player, but I did wonder why DVDs were round and not square. I never cared about how a respiratory system functions in the body, but I did seriously wonder why many of us have that small indentation between our nose and mouth. Eventually, I googled it; it's called a *philtrum*, and it's fascinating. I didn't wonder how a president came to be elected but why people would vote for him and why he'd want to run for office in the first place. The origin, the purpose, the plan behind a thing is still intriguing to me, often moreso than the execution and the evaluation of it.

Likewise, the *why* has plagued me as how I view my body has changed. In all the years I spent working on and worrying about my body, I was always been just a touch concerned and convicted that I was desiring the wrong things for the wrong reasons. And often, I was doing just that: I've desired body perfection instead of freedom, and I've desired transformation for my glory instead of His.

During that time, I was always nagged by the sneaking suspicion that I wouldn't experience true freedom and healing until I wanted it for the right reasons. I worried that I wouldn't experience restoration in my body until my *why* was acceptable to God. I remember the first time I ever allowed that worry to move from the back channels of my brain to my lips. I was in college, talking to a good friend, when it all came tumbling out.

I don't mind telling you that I was living in the midst of extreme bondage at the time. I want to honor my intention to keep this book trigger-free, so I won't expound on all the different disordered behaviors related to my body image that I engaged in. Some were plain to see and lauded as healthy by people I knew, but some were dark and quiet—hidden and hopeless. The light couldn't get in because I intentionally kept it out—a mixture of shame and seduction kept me hiding my brokenness. I was in a pit, digging deeper and deeper in the wrong direction for approval. My body was collateral damage in my quest to be someone worth knowing, someone worth loving.

Even in the pit, I could determine that there were two main wars I was waging: an inner war and an outer war. The inner war was between me and God, wrestling and wrangling over what was sin and selfishness, and what would ultimately be relinquished to Him. The outer war was the battle between me and my flesh. How would I become the picture of myself that was ideal? How would my body become "good," not just in my eyes, but in the eyes of my culture? How could I get my junk together?

In my mind, I saw a connection, but it wasn't the true connection I see today. I stood in our little college rental home, sweaty from the South Carolina summer heat, and said out loud to my friend what, until then, I'd only dared to think in my head: *"I sort of think God isn't going to let me get my body right until I get my heart right. On paper, my body should be changing—it should be performing—but I'm doing it so sinfully that I'm pretty certain God is holding out on me until my heart is pure."*

I vaguely remember her saying she'd never thought of that before. I wish my memory included me realizing how backward my theory was, how counter it was to having the mind of Christ. But eighteen years later, I'm still unraveling this false conditional statement I have believed about God: If I get my heart right, He'll make my body "right."

There are so many layers of untruth here, but let's just hit the high points:

- God can't "make my body right" because He already did. He made it good the first time.
- My heart can only get as "right" as the heart of a saint, saved by grace, in a fallen world. It will always have false motives and desires.
- God isn't in the business of rewarding spiritual righteousness with worldly success, and I am not entitled to any such expectation.

As my husband often reminds me, we don't invest in the spiritual to gain in the physical. We might pray for physical blessing, we might ask for it, we might even work in the physical for physical blessing (such as working at our jobs for money). But God cannot be tricked, He will not be mocked, and I just don't think His great plan for my life includes me looking like a Christian Barbie doll, you know? I believe He wants good for me, has good for me, and does good on my behalf—I just think the good He has and wants is so much greater than achieving the beauty standards of my culture.

In case no one has ever told you, I'd like to pause and offer you the same encouragement. I believe God wants good for your body. I believe He wants healing and restoration for you. I believe He wants freedom and wants you to experience the wholeness He purchased for you on the cross of Christ. But I don't believe that means you'll look like you've always hoped to look. I don't believe restoration is defined by experiencing the bodies we idealize here on earth; rather, I believe it's a far greater vision than that.

These days, I do believe there is a connection between the "rightness" of my body and the posture of my heart, but not at all in the way you might expect. I no longer believe that if my heart is surrendered to God, God will reward me with the body I want. Today, I believe that when my heart is surrendered to God, with Him on the throne, and His kingdom as the cornerstone of my worldview, I am able to see just how right and good my body already is.

## Why before How

These days, everyone loves talking about how to grow. I, too, love talking about how to grow. I love strategizing and planning about how to grow in every facet of my life. Let's grow spiritually! Let's grow in our leadership! Let's grow personally and collectively! I'd like to grow in my homemaking and in my ability to lead a good meeting. A few years ago, in his mid-thirties, my husband literally grew another few inches, and I was honestly super jealous. Let's grow! Let's talk about how to do it.

When I fantasize about my dream day, the best day I could ever live, it always includes a few hours of standing before a whiteboard, making a plan with someone I love. That plan, that gift of strategy that I love exercising is partnering with God to figure out the best way to grow—the best path to expand.

And I would conjecture that much of God's Word is instruction about *how* to grow. There's Luke 8, The Parable of the Sower:

> This is the meaning of the parable: The seed is the word of God. Those along the path are the ones who hear, and then the devil comes and takes away the word from their hearts, so that they may not believe and be saved. Those on the rocky ground are the ones who receive the word with joy when they hear it, but they have no root. They believe for a while, but in the time of testing they fall away. The seed that fell among thorns stands for those who hear, but as they go on their way

they are choked by life's worries, riches and pleasures, and they do not mature. But the seed on good soil stands for those with a noble and good heart, who hear the word, retain it, and by persevering produce a crop. (Luke 8:11–15)

To grow well, we need good soil. This is helpful! 2 Peter 1:5–8 gives us insight about what areas to seek growth in and how to mature spiritually:

For this very reason, make every effort to add to your faith goodness; and to goodness, knowledge; and to knowledge, self-control; and to self-control, perseverance; and to perseverance, godliness; and to godliness, mutual affection; and to mutual affection, love. For if you possess these qualities in increasing measure, they will keep you from being ineffective and unproductive in your knowledge of our Lord Jesus Christ.

Being thoughtful regarding how we grow and in what ways we grow is a beautiful and incredibly fruitful endeavor. I'm working under the assumption that you purchased this book, or began reading it, with the intention of growing and the hope of receiving information about how to do so. This is good, worthy stuff. But I've got a Jessi-ism coming your way. A sideways question you might not have considered before.

Do you know *why* you want to grow?

Let's get specific: As it pertains to having a kingdom-minded mentality, to experiencing freedom in your body, *why* do you want to grow? What is the motivation for this growth, this movement?

I'm all for the Jesus-y answers if you mean them, but I suggest we make this a brave space where we can all unzip and be honest about the desires of our hearts. In order to lead well, I'll go first and tell you a few inclinations I've found roaming around in my own mind.

*I desire to work on my body image because I want other people to think I'm OK. I believe I won't seem as broken if this part of me is fixed.*

We'll come back to that. While I'm feeling resolute, I'll get another one out:

*I want to work on my body image because I perceive it will make me more desirable. If I'm free, healthy, and confident, other people will want to know me and be around me.*

And finally:

*I desire to be at ease. I want to get my heart and body in alignment with God's will so I can finally take a deep breath and live at ease with who I am.*

What's the point in asking such in-depth questions about *why* we want to grow? Why pull this thread and examine our hearts with such intensity? I promise it's not because I want to wallow in morbid introspection, but rather it's because I've found that misplaced desires and motives keep me from seeing the abundance, healing, and freedom *I already have*. It's the motivations that are *not* rooted in the truth of God that have kept me from restoration. And if I believe that God created my body good, then I'm not working to make my body good but endeavoring to see it restored to its original creation.

A few days ago, I let myself name these deviated desires and motives in the privacy of my journal. Divulging my motives (good or bad) is one of my favorite pastimes, and I've found that honesty with God often leads to discovering the abundance that has been there all along. When I've gone into the secret place and poured out my heart to Him, no matter how terrifying it is, the refreshment that comes usually wells up out of my mouth and into my life. I can't keep the healing that comes from being heard by Him inside, and the confession of my healing produces fruit. Asking *why* I want to grow often leads me to *how* I can grow. You feel me?

After naming my motivations out loud to God, I felt prompted by the Holy Spirit to speak truth to the desires of my heart. And that's when I felt myself shifting. Here's what I wrote:

To the desire to seem like you're OK: Jess, you're already OK. You've already been OK. You have been created in love and redeemed in promise by God. You will never graduate from needing the gospel, but when God looks at you, He sees Jesus. And you're free! You're whole! You're healed! You still live under the effects of this fallen world, so you may not feel like it, but God isn't holding out on you.

To the desire to be desired: You already are. The God who created the universe paid the price of His Son so that you could be brought near to Him. He loves you, and He loves time with you. The truest thing about you will always be that you are loved by Him. No human desire could ever measure up to His eager devotion and inclination to be close to you.

To the desire to be at ease: You can be. By grace through faith, you can be wrapped in the security of your Father. But while you live on this earth, you're never going to feel totally at home. It's always going to feel a little bit foreign. You may as well give up the fight and get used to missing heaven, because that's the place you were made for.

Simply by naming these desires and speaking truth to them, I've realized that paying attention to *why* I want to grow and addressing that *why* can be incredibly fruitful. And what's more, when I identify what is prompting me to expand and develop, I realize, *Look at that! I'm already growing.* And it's not that I'm becoming someone new, someone stronger, someone better—it's that I'm coming back to the truth of God that lives in me. I'm being restored.

## We Don't Need Your Tent Here

Jesus' disciples were classic *how* and *what* type guys. They often missed the *why*, and it seemed to grieve Jesus. The *what* was their mission, the undeniably important task they'd been given of making other disciples and bringing the kingdom of heaven to earth. The *how* ranged from healing people to preaching to providing food and even utilizing prayer. The *why* was because He is worthy of worship. *Why?* Because He is the son of God. *Why?* Because He loves us and brings us to His Father.

I like to picture Jesus' frustration when I read about them getting it wrong and picture what kind of face He made. In Matthew 16, when Jesus calls Peter "Satan," I'm guessing the annoyance level was through the roof. Like maybe level 12 out of 10? I can imagine Jesus taking a deep breath and looking heavenward when, in Matthew 18, the disciples start arguing about who will be honored most in heaven. I'm guessing 9.3 out of 10 for that time. Can you imagine Him? Deep breath in, deep breath out. Silently looking up to heaven and praying, "Dad? For real with these guys?" When He most likely felt like screaming at them, Jesus motions for a child to join them while He calmly preaches about humility and the kingdom of heaven.

But between these two frustrating moments, there's another that's wildly fascinating to me—the Mount of Transfiguration.

Jesus is in the thick of His earthly ministry. He is healing people, He is teaching a lot, and He has already predicted His death. He's traveling with these twelve appointed disciples and a host of others who have latched on to him. He occasionally

135

breaks away with one or a few of the disciples—to teach them something specific and poignant. He has one-on-one interactions with people that are recorded because they're meaningful for all of us. And then, in Matthew 17, He invites Peter, James, and John to go up on a mountain with Him. We can guess from their recorded location that it was Mount Tabor in Israel.

There, on the mountain, Jesus allows his disciples to see him transformed into a version of Himself more full of glory than they'd previously seen. His face shone, and His clothes became as white as the light. They got a special glimpse of the glory of God through their friend Jesus that no one else had ever seen. But there was more! Not only did they see Jesus in all his holy splendor, but Elijah and Moses were also there before them. Two saints who'd been dead for hundreds of years, heroes to the disciples, appeared before them.

Can you pause right now and imagine how you'd respond if you saw Jesus in all His glory, flanked by two long-dead heroes of the faith? Would you fall down in worship? Grab a camera? Start asking questions? Peter had another idea:

> Peter said to Jesus, "Lord, it is good for us to be here. If you wish, I will put up three shelters—one for you, one for Moses and one for Elijah."
>
> While he was still speaking, a bright cloud covered them, and a voice from the cloud said, "This is my Son, whom I love; with him I am well pleased. Listen to him!"
>
> When the disciples heard this, they fell facedown to the ground, terrified. But Jesus came and touched them. "Get up," he said. "Don't be afraid." When they looked up, they saw no one except Jesus. (Matt. 17:4–8)

We'll come back to Peter's suggestion about building tents in a moment. This is a mysterious scene, to be sure, but there are at least a few reasons I'm grateful we get to read about it:

1. I'm grateful we're reminded through the appearance of Elijah and Moses, the audible voice of God the Father, and the glory of the Holy Spirit that our God is not separate from the God of the Israelites. The Trinity has been one from the beginning, Jesus was not absent from the Old Testament (though He is fully revealed in the New Testament), and our God is the same God worshipped by these heroes of the faith.

2. I'm grateful He took the disciples in the midst of their confusion and *showed* their souls what their brains could not quite compute. I'm grateful God knows and adjusts to our limitations. When our faith fails us, and we need to experience something with our own eyes, He provides. I bet they remembered the experience for the rest of their lives.

3. Finally, I'm grateful for this one sentence from our Father via the cloud above them: "This is my Son, whom I love; with him I am well pleased. Listen to him!" (Matt. 17:5).

Did you notice how, just before that moment, Peter defaults to *what* he can do for God in the midst of being shown an incredible *why*? We have *Jesus*, full of glory and splendor, talking to *Moses* and *Elijah*. And instead of falling on his knees to worship—the ultimate *why*—Peter is trying to set up camp. Peter is tempted to *do something* when he could simply be in awe of *Someone*. He's skipped right over *why* this matters and is instead thinking about *what* to do, perhaps because doing is too often our default mode. But Jesus didn't want Peter to *do* anything; He simply wanted him to witness and worship.

I read this passage a few weeks into writing this book, a few weeks into asking God to heal my *why* for seeing my body as good, when I realized I've spent most of my adult life being like Peter: *doing* when God is inviting me to simply *be* with Him in worship.

I've been placed in this miraculously-made-good physical body, created by the One who crafted the mountains, the seas, the clouds, and everything in between. Every single detail of my body has been carved with intention, then upheld by His hand in the midst of a fallen and failing world. In Luke 12, Jesus Himself says He knows exactly the number of hairs on my head. What's more, the power that raised Him from the dead has been placed inside me so I can accomplish His will here on earth. My soul has been brought from darkness to light, purchased with the blood of Christ so I can live forever and tell as many people about Him as possibly on my way to eternity.

Is this not reason enough to worship?

I wake up every morning and see that the earth has not yet fallen away. The sun has risen, the day has come despite the effects of death and destruction all around us. I get to move this body, loving, serving, seeing the hand and hope of God. I get to use my hands, my feet, and my mouth to do His work.

On top of all that, I continue to grow. I'm able to perceive conviction and my need for repentance, and my soul is never stagnant but shifts as He leads me. My relationships shift and change and become more whole. My life of mission ebbs and flows; I find passion and rest and purpose and all the good things God brings to fruition when I act in obedience. I see prayers answered; I see hearts changed when they aren't answered the way we hope. I see other people change. I see shifts in culture. I breathe—in and out, over and over—as I commune with God and long for heaven.

I am living in a miracle. It's not the Mount of Transfiguration, but it's still incredible. I live in the world, but I also live in the kingdom, and my good body carries me through it all. And yet, like Peter, I look down at my physical circumstances and become obsessed with shelter. I get hung up on my physical body, even with God's abundance available to me. When I do, I miss out on seeing Jesus and listening to Him. I miss the worship opportunity that's right at my feet. I miss the memo straight from the mouth of God: *"This is my Son, whom I love; with him I am well pleased. Listen to him!"*

Listen to him when He says your body is good.

Listen to him when He says you are meant for restoration.

Listen to him when He says the shelter is not the main event here—far from it—and when He invites us to behold the glory of Jesus instead of getting tripped up by our earthly bodies.

When we think about our bodies, we often think about *how* we can make them better. Behind that endeavor, there's likely a myriad of motives worth paying attention to. *Why* we want to treat our bodies better or, at the least, learn to see them from God's perspective isn't always cut and dried. Many of us have bought into lies about our bodies that infect us and our intentions with negativity.

I'm proposing a new *why* to drive our efforts as we seek restoration for our bodies. I'm offering a new *why* for restoration, one that is far more sustainable and motivating than any *why* aimed at self-betterment for self-betterment's sake.

There are a million potential *whys* behind wanting health, beauty, and betterment for our bodies. But what if we recalibrated them all to affirm the ultimate *why*—to break free from shame and experience the abundance of God in our bodies? What if our *why* became less about pleasing people, achieving cultural expectations, even breaking a new personal best for health and wellness, and more about saying yes and amen to the growth God wants for us? What if our driving mission, our deepest *why*, was no longer about trying to prove ourselves but about seeing what God can do and giving Him glory?

I believe the path we are all on, the path to loving our bodies the way God would, is an individual Mount of Transfiguration for each of us. I believe this endeavor to function in a kingdom body mentality is an opportunity to see Jesus in a way that will change our lives forever. I perceive He wants to show us parts and pieces of Himself that we've never seen before. I perceive He wants us to show us parts and pieces of Himself *in us* that we've never seen before. Let's not stand before Him in all His glory and ask if we should be fixing our tents instead of listening to Him. Let's pay attention to our motives and set our intentions on this one thing as we grow in the way we view our bodies, experiencing the love, freedom, and goodness of God as we grow. Amen?

> For we know that if the earthly tent we live in is destroyed, we have a building from God, an eternal house in heaven, not built by human hands. Meanwhile we groan, longing to be clothed instead with our heavenly dwelling, because when we are clothed, we will not be found naked. For while we are in this tent, we groan and are burdened, because we do not wish to be unclothed but to be clothed instead with our heavenly dwelling, so that what is mortal may be swallowed up by life. Now the one who has fashioned us for this very purpose is God, who has given us the Spirit as a deposit, guaranteeing what is to come. (2 Cor. 5:1–5)

What if, every time you encounter a feeling about wanting your body to be better, to be different, you ask Jesus to help you see Him and restore how you see yourself? What if, every time a memory of shame or significant disappointment hits, you ask Him for a kingdom-minded perspective? What if you declare war on the enemy of your soul, who wants you to think your body is a trophy, a marker of your righteousness, or a project to be completed, and you decide instead that your body is a place to see the goodness and glory of God restored and displayed?

What if, even on the days when you feel the most shame or pain or frustration with your body become times when you allow Him to comfort and connect with you? What if your best days in your body are moments to give Him praise and thanks? What if you discovered you have a partner in the journey of seeing your body as good, and what if that partner is Jesus?

## Now, the How

Our *why* for growing in our perspective of our bodies is to experience God. We're in this thing to see more of Him. We've broken ties with the agreement that our bodies are projects or that they're up for appraisal by the world. We're not going to grow because we want to be better, to be loved, or to be more holy. We're here because He's here, and we want to experience Him as much as we can. That's our *why*. Now we get to talk about *how* we'll grow.

Raise your hand if you thought that, perhaps, somewhere in this book there'd be a short list or a plan or, at the very least, a handful of action steps to help you take better care of your body. No shame. Nobody can see you raising your hand. You're safe.

The bad news is, I don't have any of these things for you. The good news is, your body is *already* good—full stop.

Your body lives in the kingdom, and recognizing that frees you from the captivity of this world while also calling you to the existence of an eternal one. Your body has been named by God and can be renamed as good by you, even after years or decades of defamation by those who meant harm. Your body can rest;

you can take a deep breath and stop participating in cycles of improving, tinkering, and provoking your body. But to experience restoration—to partner with God in moving forward, to begin treating your body as good—you don't need a list or a plan. At least, I don't perceive that those are the greatest things that will serve you.

You need worship. The *why* and the *how* are so closely linked—it will make perfect sense when you see it.

The *why* behind this work of body image is to experience God more, so naturally, the *how* is worshipping Him. Our old *why* may have been to get better or to earn other people's approval, and thus, our *how* was to provoke our bodies and make them into projects. But when the goal is to experience God, the action steps all lead us into His presence to take what we need. It's simple *and* it's life-giving. Let's be reminded about the power of worship:

> Therefore, I urge you, brothers and sisters, in view of God's mercy, to offer your bodies as a living sacrifice, holy and pleasing to God—this is your true and proper worship. Do not conform to the pattern of this world, but be transformed by the renewing of your mind. Then you will be able to test and approve what God's will is—his good, pleasing and perfect will. (Rom. 12:1–2)

Worship is the healing our bodies need. When we are enthralled by the glory of God, we will start seeing everything else in its proper light. But what does that look like fleshed out? For the purpose of moving forward with clarity and conviction, let's define what we mean.

Worship is any act that allows us to be more in awe of God, more aware of God, or creates a space for us to give Him praise. I believe our eating can be worship. I believe our exercise can be worship. I believe our resting can be worship. I believe our work can be worship. I also believe that all of those things can easily *not* be worship. It's up to us to shift our hearts and minds.

We're going to flesh this out more in the last few chapters, but for now, let's dig back into the passage from Romans to compare our current reality with the benchmark of worship.

1. *Start in view of God's mercy.* For any lasting change and progress to be made in our lives, His character must be the catalyst. If we're trying to *earn* His love or our place in the kingdom, it won't work. If we're trying to make the world happy, it won't work. Or maybe it will appear to "work," but we'll be exhausted from striving rather than feeling connected from abiding. But when we start with God's mercy and love and grace as our motivation, we're compelled to keep coming to Him for more insight. We're reminded of how much we need Him, so we don't run ahead too quickly and lose steam. If you're looking for any kind of a plan, the mercy of God—the truth that He has compassion and care for you—is an incredible place to start.

2. *Offer your body to God.* This is where we check our motives, where we experience restoration in our intentions. Are we seeking renewal or growth because we want to offer ourselves to the world and be found good? Are we fussing with our bodies so that we can be counted as beautiful? Are we trying to do this apart from the grace, the presence, and the power of God? Do we think we can trick Him or outsmart Him? Are we hiding from Him? Or are we acknowledging that He is our King, our bodies are His good creation, and we're walking with Him on this path of restoration?

3. *This is your true and proper worship.* Have you ever entertained the idea that you could worship with Him as

you wrestle with this issue in your heart? Have you ever stopped in the midst of a moment wherein you're experiencing frustration and heartbreak over your body and sought His face in order to find your soul? As I've said, I believe the journey we're on with our bodies can be our ultimate Mount of Transfiguration—the place where we open our eyes and see the glory of God revealed in the midst of our fallenness. I believe that when we look at Him in awe, when we live our lives in an effort to please and praise Him, not only do our hearts change, but the way we perceive the world around us also shifts.

4. *Do not conform to the pattern of this world.* This may be one of the most essential parts of the "plan," if you can call worshipping a plan. To really honor and exult the King of Kings, we often have to lay down the trappings of man-made culture we've been tied to in the past, even the things that have made us feel safe, secure, and like we're doing the right thing.

   I will give you a small example that is honest and real for me. In writing this book, in seeking to fully function in a kingdom body mentality, God asked me to stop weighing myself daily. It was a rhythm, a part of the "plan" that had "worked" for me for my whole life. And yet, upon worshipping God and giving Him back my body, asking Him for restoration—I realize that weighing myself was a pattern of the world that distracted me from praising Him and listening to Him about my body. Will I ever weigh myself again? I imagine so. Do I have other patterns to break free from? Absolutely. Will new patterns arise that I will need to break from in the future? I'd be willing to bet on it. This kind of transformation is an ongoing process.

5. *Be transformed by the renewing of your mind.* Let me ask you

this: Are you open to God changing your mind? Is God allowed to change your mind, not just once, but in an ongoing process to help you see yourself and the world the way He does? Do you want to think about yourself and others the way God does? Are you willing to work at that—capturing the ideas you have held to, holding them up to His truth, and shifting them so your life can be continually made new?

Is God allowed to change your mind about whether or not your body is good? Is God allowed to change your mind about what a good body looks like? Is God allowed to change your mind about what it looks like to actively love and care for your good body? If He's not allowed to change our minds, I'd argue that our connection with Him is not worship. And if it's not worship, we can't experience restoration.

6. *Then, you'll see what His perfect will is for you.* You'll get to view the plan that's specific to *you*. Worship is a way forward in regard to loving our bodies, and it's at our fingertips. It's doable for those of us who are in Christ Jesus. I would even venture to say it isn't difficult, because communing with God is what we were made to do. But while it's not difficult, it isn't *simple*. Worship is not a one-and-done situation, and it's also not elementary. To be motivated by His grace and mercy and submit this area of our lives (our bodies) to God out of reverence for Him is not simple. To become more in awe of Him than frustrated with ourselves, to forsake following the culture and allow Him to change our minds—that's not *simple*. It's going to take supernatural strength. It may also take our whole lives.

But, what really, is our choice? The various paths that culture provides may, at first glance, appear to be helpful—at least toward meeting our physical goals—but they're not healing *us*. Even when our bodies are changing, our hearts are crying out for freedom and hope. As daughters of God whose souls were made to sing His praise, why not try worship as our way forward? This is what we were made to do.

I'm not naive enough to think that telling you to worship will solve all your problems. My body, which I absolutely believe is made good, is complicated. I've learned over the years that loving her and taking care of her is not simple. She needs rest, she needs certain foods, she needs to move, she needs healing from years of damage I've done and from my environment. My body needs support from my mind, my soul, and my surroundings.

In going with God, worshipping on my way, I have discovered He is a generous, kind, and gracious God. When the compassionate people in my life (it happens even with those who are the most loving) have lost interest or capacity to care about what's happening with my body, God doesn't. He keeps listening and giving me insight. No matter what the subject is, the Holy Spirit is a better communicator and teacher and coach than any human ever could be.

When you live in worship, you love what God loves and start to see everything the way He does, *including your body*. Worship teaches us to love and care for our bodies as God does—to experience them with gratitude and patience and kindness as we exchange our worldly perspective for His kingdom one. Picture a time you went into a worship gathering with a disgruntled heart or mind and had your position shifted for the better. If we are willing to accept the invitation, God will shift our hearts, changing how we feel about our bodies as we use them and care for them.

Maybe you are desperate for a *how*. Maybe you need an immediate plan of action to love your body well, to treat it with kindness and hope, to cease causing it harm and to welcome its healing. Many of us need human guides on the way—doctors, therapists, nutritionists, trainers. I've gotten help from all of these experts, and I've been grateful for it. I just pray that as we go, as we move forward, we also worship. I pray we keep the King at the focus of our freedom. I pray He gets an intimate invitation to see our progression, to guide our way. I pray that as we grow in loving our bodies, we're able to worship.

I believe many of us may come to this work wanting to be better, to be someone new, to grow past or out of our current realities. But the restoration we experience when we worship is what our souls and our communities need most.

# Questions

Have you ever thought about **why** you want healing or restoration in your body?

Why do you want to grow?

What if living in your body was less about how you could make it better and more about seeing God?

When you eat, when you move, when you spend time in your body, are you more in awe of God? Are you aware of Him at all?

What would an act of worship in your body, outside of the typical singing and dancing, look like today?

# Words from Our Friends

**Sarah:** *A couple of years ago, my church gave away cacti and small succulents instead of flowers for Mother's Day. I took home a tiny cactus, but because of my previous track record with plants, I expected it to die within weeks. However, I am apparently a great cactus mother. I watered it sparingly and watched it grow, eventually transferring it to a big pot to watch it grow even more. It's been two years since I first repotted that cactus, and earlier this year, it flowered, bearing a big, beautiful, yellow flower.*

*At the same time I adopted the cactus, I had started some serious counseling work on my history of body image issues and disordered eating. It felt like God was telling me, "Growth takes time. Keep at it. You will bloom, too." Sometimes I just need a visual to remember that I'm growing even when I don't feel God doing the gardening. I needed the reminder that it's because He loves us that He puts so much work and time into helping us grow, even when we don't see it.*

# CHAPTER 8

# Your Body Is Not a Marker of Righteousness

*Let's get an iced mocha oat milk latte and talk.*

If I could, I would grab your arm today and we'd go for a walk down the block to get some coffee, because I have something to tell you.

As I write this, it's a Saturday. I get up early and write, then, as a family, we spend some time at the church getting it prepped for Sunday, do chores around the house, and then hang and rest together. But sometimes, while the kids are doing chores, I can sneak away for a coffee.

If you were with me, I'd suggest we meet at The Harbinger, which is just a block away from my home and boasts the most beautiful indoor color scheme of dusty pink, faded blue, and greige. I'd get an iced mocha oat milk latte—the one from Harb is amazing. I'm strictly a black coffee girl, except on Saturday afternoons when the day has started off kind of weird.

Then we'd snag a table in the corner and, while you're blowing on your coffee to cool it, I'd tell you this story:

I should know better than to open Instagram before I write. I feel like I should know better than to open Instagram unless God has prompted me to check on someone or use the internet to encourage someone. But today, I broke my own rules and had my phone right beside my bed. I rolled over to grab it before I got up and saw that someone had aggressively (or passive-aggressively) tagged me in over a dozen posts. It was clear there was something this person wanted me to see.

They were Botox ads. Someone, overnight, tagged me in the comments of dozens of Instagram Botox ads. I clicked on the username of the person who did the tagging. It was not a random internet bully. No, it was a woman from my city. I don't follow her, but she's a friend of friends. This real live human, who lives in my city and knows my friends, took it upon herself to tag me in various Botox ads between the hours of 11 p.m. and 6 a.m., presumably to (a) inform me that I need Botox and (b) let me know where I can get it.

It's not the first time this has happened. For whatever reason, people on Instagram often suggest I should get Botox. I have an expressive face, and when I talk on Instagram Stories, those little wrinkles are all you can see. But it's been a few months since it last happened, and it's never before been someone who is a friend of a friend.

At this point in our afternoon coffee date, whether or not I cry is going to depend a lot on your reaction. If you're laughing, I'll laugh. If you're sitting quietly and looking at me with shock and sadness, I might tear up. If you act like it's not a big deal and say something like, "Good! Tell me where to get it. I've been meaning to tell you that you could use a few units on your forehead!" I may walk out. Because you and I are too far into this journey of calling our bodies good to put that kind of crazy on each other, OK?

The point of this is not the Botox. I'm not anti-Botox, and if you've had Botox, more power to you. I was dead set on getting it a few years ago—like money in hand, doctor picked out. Then, my older sister lovingly entreated me to keep my forehead wrinkles intact because, she said, my face is "so expressive," and she didn't want it to change. She made a big case about Julia Roberts and how expressive her face is and how she says publicly that she doesn't get Botox (on the real, I think she does). My point is: my beef is not with Botox.

My beef is not even with pristine foreheads popping up around the Western Hemisphere, but rather with the expectation that women who meet a certain set of beauty standards are inherently *better* than women who don't.

## What I Wish They'd Said

I was thirty when I sat in a small circle with two other women who were about seven years older than me. I esteemed them more than I could express, but I was trying not to notice those feelings at the moment. I was trying to play it cool—to "act like I've been there," as my husband would say. Both women had reached a level in their careers that I hoped to achieve one day. They were both leading large teams and teaching all over the country. These two heroes of mine were women on mission using all they've got for the good of others and the glory of God.

At one point in the conversation, one where I was intentionally on the fringes (*Play it cool, Connolly—don't be overzealous and ask 304 questions*), the subject wound around to Botox. They began discussing where they got it and how many CCs they got, and I just sat in their midst, doe-eyed and quiet. As much as I can recall how I felt emotionally, I don't think I felt judgmental or disappointed in them—just confused about what they were saying. But maybe my silence felt like something else to them, because one of these women turned to me and said, "You don't get it. You'll need it one day soon! Just wait! It's a work expense for sure."

A few years later, I had my next run-in with the B word. A friend of mine had recently been invited to record the announcements her church played before and after services. After her first stint, one of the deacons called to check in on her, telling her what a good job she had done, but also passing along the number of a local dermatologist who could help her out with some Botox. He had been appointed to communicate that, "With those HD screens, it would honestly be a really good investment! It would only aid in your communication skills if other opportunities present themselves."

Now, first of all, I'd like to remember that Satan is the enemy, and I'd like to have a conversation with the enemy of our souls right now. *Satan, can you get off our foreheads? Like, for real? Right now. Just go back to hell. You already came for our butts and our breasts. You came for our teeth and our bellies, and Lord knows you've tried to come for our hair. But our foreheads? You've got women cutting bangs and spending good money on the few inches of skin between their eyes and hairlines and it's just getting crazy. In the name of Jesus, please go somewhere else and get off our foreheads.*

OK, now here's what I want to say to you:

I've made it my life's work the last few years to be a coach and a champion of people. I don't like to call them out or correct them. Instead, I relish the joy of calling God's people *up* and reminding them who He made them to be. But sometimes you have to call an untruth what it is, and this, too, can be a way of calling God's daughters up to who they're designed to be.

Looking back, I wish that as I was sitting in that small circle of leaders I esteemed so highly, they would have turned to me and spoken shame off me (and themselves!), instead of speaking shame on me and my inevitable future wrinkles. I wish they'd spoken words of truth about how God equips those He calls, and I wish they'd said something about how the qualification for ministry is a heart that pleases God, not a face that fits in with the worldly standards of beauty. I wish the three of us could have banded together for a moment of vulnerable victory, declaring war against the cultural expectations that were fighting their way into our church, into our sense of the kingdom. I wish that's how that moment had gone, instead of me staying silent and playing it cool and letting that lie have the last word.

I also wish that when that deacon called my friend a few years ago, he had thanked her for being brave in front of tens of thousands of people. I wish they looked for older women to speak to their congregation as well, no matter how aged their faces. I sometimes wish men were leading this conversation, and with repentance, because they've been complicit in the cultural movement to hold women to the lie that they have to meet certain standards of beauty in order to make an impact for the Lord.

I wish all those moments could have gone differently, along with all the other millions of moments we've experienced—moments wherein lay the possibility for commissioning but instead, condemnation, shame, and embarrassment abounded. I think about the millions of private moments wherein a woman has had a sense of what obedience in ministry or mission or life could look like for her, but has been paralyzed because her body, or the perception others have of it, feels disqualifying.

## Does God Talk like This?

I have met many, many women who feel disqualified from stepping into the good things God has for them because of their bodies. I have met many, many women who feel they cannot possibly ask God for the things they want because they believe their bodies disqualify them. A new season, a new relationship, a new spiritual gift, the feeling of freedom, children, promotion, and even friendship—these are a few of the things we believe we are not entitled to until our bodies are at least somewhat close to the cultural standard.

I want to acknowledge that these are what I call "back-of-the-mind thoughts." We may not say them out loud; they may simply be unacknowledged assumptions that we live with. Others of us may have actually said these things out loud or made agreements with these lies. We may have been told these untruths from an early age, making it all the more difficult for us to break free of them.

But before we move any further, because I trust you—and the Holy Spirit in you—so much, I want to pause and invite you to answer this question:

Once we say these things out loud, in light of all we've discussed about having a kingdom-minded view of our bodies, *do these conditional statements concerning the callings on our lives sound like something God would endorse?*

Let's shake our heads for a moment, dusting off the cultural confines and even lies we've been told, and ask, *Does God talk like this?*

Would the God we know and love, the God who created and sustains us, say:

*You can't enter the next phase of your life until your body fits the
culture's expectation.*
*You can't have access to the spiritual gift I gave you until you
look better.*
*You can't have the children, family, or relationship I planned for
you until you get your body business in order.*

I vote no. I hate even writing those sentences because I
believe they are wrong and far from the heart of God. And yet I
can't tell you how many times I've heard someone claim to speak
for God, applying those untruths to Him and from Him.

Often, in a discipleship moment, when I'm meeting with a
gal from church or someone I'm leading, I'll encourage a woman
to physically respond with the truth that she believes. Something
about putting our beliefs in motion helps us remember that they
are true. For example, when a woman comes up against the lie
that her body disqualifies her from God's abundance, I'll encourage her to shake her head in an active, definitive *no* response.
Sometimes it takes a few tries. Sometimes our misunderstanding
of the gospel is rooted so deeply, it takes relearning His Word
to realize He never expected, demanded, or asked for perfection
from us. Rather, He anticipated our great need for grace and
mercy and provided a rescue in the way of Jesus.

> Therefore, there is now no condemnation for those who are in
> Christ Jesus. (Rom. 8:1)

If God Himself declared the war of condemnation against
our souls over, why would we continually attribute this condemn-
ing, conditional message to Him?

Let's look a little more closely at the best passage in Scripture
regarding God's image of our bodies versus the world's image.

## Look at This, Not That

The people of God, the Israelites, had been through it all. God had established them out of Jacob, renamed Israel—the man who wrestled with God. Jacob had twelve sons, each of whom became the forefather of his own tribe. The family of Jacob grew in Egypt until it became so large, the people posed a threat to Pharaoh, and much conflict ensued. God appointed Moses to lead them out of slavery and to the land He'd promised to their forefather, Abraham. That exodus became a forty-year journey into the wilderness. Moses died, and his predecessor, Joshua, led them over the Jordan River and into the promised land. For several hundred years, the people lived under the rule of their priests and judges.

The Israelites were constantly under threat, despite being God's chosen people. The nations surrounding them were intimidating and warlike, and their own sinful behavior made them vulnerable.

Samuel, a well-respected prophet and priest, comes on the scene in this season, but before we recall what he did, it's important to remember one important fact about Samuel: *he listened to God.*

Samuel's mother, Hannah, longed for a child. She made a vow that if God would give her a son, she would give him back in service to God. After Samuel was weaned, he was sent to the temple to learn how to serve God and His people. Samuel grew up in the temple during a season when Israel's leaders failed to honor the Lord, instead using the position of leadership for their own gain. Samuel, however, relentlessly listened to God.

He listened when he was just a boy and heard the audible voice of God calling him in the night (1 Sam. 3). And he listened when God told him to give the Israelites the king they were asking for, even though they wanted a king for the wrong reasons:

> When Samuel heard their demand—"Give us a king to rule us!"—he was crushed. How awful! Samuel prayed to GOD.
>
> GOD answered Samuel, "Go ahead and do what they're asking. They are not rejecting you. They've rejected me as their King. From the day I brought them out of Egypt until this very day they've been behaving like this, leaving me for other gods. And now they're doing it to you. So let them have their own way. But warn them of what they're in for. Tell them the way kings operate, just what they're likely to get from a king."
>
> But the people wouldn't listen to Samuel. "No!" they said. "We will have a king to rule us! Then we'll be just like all the other nations. Our king will rule us and lead us and fight our battles."
>
> Samuel took in what they said and rehearsed it with GOD. GOD told Samuel, "Do what they say. Make them a king." (1 Sam. 8:6–9, 19–22 MSG)

Shortly after that, Samuel listened when God selected Saul, a handsome guy who seemed unlikely to lead well, to be king of Israel (1 Sam. 9). The Word of God tells us that Saul was good-looking and a head taller than most people, but history tells us how unlikely he was as a choice. He came from the smallest, most insignificant tribe of Israel. And he was looking for lost donkeys, not power and glory, when God pointed him out to Samuel.

Saul's humble beginnings didn't keep him from a prideful end. Samuel listened to God again when he had to tell Saul he would be replaced by a man after God's heart (1 Sam. 13). Saul had a bad habit of doing what God asked him to do but improvising when and how it suited him. It was after one of those times that Samuel declared,

> "You have done a foolish thing . . . You have not kept the command the LORD your God gave you; if you had, he would have established your kingdom over Israel for all time. But now your kingdom will not endure; the LORD has sought out a man after his own heart and appointed him ruler of his people, because you have not kept the LORD's command." (1 Sam. 13:13–14)

Just a short while later, God told Samuel to quit mourning the loss of Saul and go get the new guy He'd chosen to be king. Saul could have killed Samuel for treason at that point, but God gave him specific instructions to go to Jesse in Bethlehem, where God would "show him what to do."

Who was Jesse? He wasn't wealthy or powerful by cultural standards. He was a farmer and a sheep breeder in the countryside. But his history was rich, and his future had been prophesied. His granddad was Boaz, the kinsman redeemer who is the hero of the Book of Ruth. And in Isaiah 11, it had been prophesied that the Messiah (the Savior of God's people) would descend from the shoot, or the root of Jesse. Jesse's future was abundant not just because of what was about to happen with Samuel, but because Jesus Christ would be descended from the line of Jesse on his mother's side.

So, historically, what we're working with here is this: Saul was handsome, but he was rejected by God because he didn't listen and obey. Jesse was a regular guy with nothing spectacular about his life, except that God had proved Himself faithful and true to Jesse's family and had promised glory for his future. These stories clearly demonstrate that the outward trappings of your life are not the way God measures you. How you look and how you're perceived by the culture around you does not bear consequence on how God treats you. Full stop.

God is about to drive this point home, so let's keep listening. Samuel went to Bethlehem, as God instructed, to offer a sacrifice. He invited Jesse and his sons, and even consecrated them—blessing them and marking them as set apart and different from everyone else. He saw Jesse's oldest son, Eliab, tall and good-looking, and assumed—he must be the new king. But—wait for it—what does God say?

> But the LORD said to Samuel, "Do not consider his appearance or his height, for I have rejected him. The LORD does not look at the things people look at. People look at the outward appearance, but the LORD looks at the heart." (1 Sam. 16:7)

The Lord looks at the heart.
The Lord looks at the heart.
The Lord looks at the heart.

I'm going to say it one more time, because we've heard and seen the opposite displayed for the entirety of our lives: *the Lord looks at the heart.*

Let's fast forward to the fact that David was no perfect king. He was an accomplice in murder, he used his power for sexual coercion, and he didn't even repent until called on it outright. He was not sinless, and he did not lead with impeccable character at all times. But.

The Lord looks at the heart.
The Lord looks at the heart.
The Lord looks at the heart.

The wild hope for us is this: not only does God not *look* at our bodies, but even our physical behavior—how we use our bodies—doesn't determine the final say. It doesn't cancel out His proclamation of love and grace toward us. When God looks at the hearts, of those of us who are followers of Jesus, He sees the righteousness of His own Son. He sees our kingdom potential and the purity with which He made us. And because He loves us, He holds us accountable and corrects us (as He did David), but He is not making a snap judgement based on what humans see.

It isn't your body, your beauty, or your behavior that God uses to determine His love for you. And it's time for us to get into agreement with the way God looks at His people.

## What Size Was Eve? (It's Not What Matters)

In all of my reading and study of Scripture, I've never found a verse that states God measures people by how they look. Instead, when the full gospel of Jesus Christ is unpacked for us in the New Testament, David's story makes even more sense to me. It's not just that God doesn't measure us by how we look; He also doesn't measure us by how we *perform*.

In the kingdom, people who have done complicated, complicit, and criminal things can have their hearts changed by God and be used in mighty ways for the good of others and the glory of God. Because the Lord looks at the heart.

In the face of sexism and racism in the cultural moment in which Jesus lived, Jesus consistently showed honor to and bestowed value upon those the world slighted and cast aside. Because the Lord looks at the heart.

In Scripture, there is no mention of Mary Magdalene's thighs, Deborah's teeth, Ruth's waistline, Anna the prophetess's forehead, Elizabeth's stretch marks, Eve's hair, Lois's skin,

Martha's tunic size, or the symmetry (or lack thereof) of Miriam's face. Because the Lord looks at the heart.

These women's faithfulness was not defined by their bodies, their capacity to be used by God was not defined by their bodies, and their bodies were never the most interesting or compelling part of their story. Because the Lord looks at the heart.

Never once did an angel go to Naomi and tell her God would be more likely to work through her if she took better care of herself. I do not believe Paul pulled Priscilla aside and told her she'd make a better missionary if she did something more special with her hair. Zipporah, the wife of Moses, is not remembered because she was stunning but because she loved a complicated man through a historically harrowing season. Because the Lord looks at the heart.

God used these women to shape the landscape of hope, healing, mercy, and meaning that we would ultimately step into as followers of Jesus. Their bodies were made good by a Creator who loved them. Their lives were valuable because they were His daughters. Their stories were stepping stones for others to get to God, not because they fit the physical cultural expectations of their time, but because they were faithful and allowed themselves to be used by God.

Because the Lord looks at the heart.

If someone (including you) has told you that your body must change in order for you to be used by God, please direct them to the story of David. If someone has told you that in order to receive the blessings God has for you, you must choose cultural conformity, tell them what God said to Samuel. If anyone has alluded, in any way, shape, or form, to a connection between your worth and value in the kingdom of God and the world's approval of your body, tell them they are dead wrong.

We live in the kingdom. And the Lord looks at the heart.

Your body is not a marker of righteousness, and it cannot and will not be used by God to determine your worth. What's more, it should not be used by anyone else to determine your goodness, readiness, or value in the kingdom or on earth.

## Talking Back to Body Shame

Let's go ahead and answer the arguments that may be entering your mind or which may have been presented to you in the past. Lord knows I've tried and heard a variety of arguments. I'd rather we be prepared to fight them with wisdom, truth, and clarity as opposed to defensiveness and fear.

I once heard that when a stronghold is being threatened, whether it exists within an individual or a culture, it gets louder and more aggressive. In this case, the stronghold that says we have to meet cultural standards of beauty in order to be used by God does just that. When you confront this kind of lie, the rebuttals are often nastier and more vindictive than the original accusation. We're going to address just one of these rebuttals, but I pray that the wisdom we use applies to any and all counterclaims you are faced with when stepping into the truth of God as it pertains to your body.

*"But you should take care of your body. If you're just letting yourself go, that isn't honoring God."*

I'm going to work through this as though you and I are back in the coffee shop together. Let's go grab another iced latte so we've got the energy to process this. Here are some truths to anchor you the next time someone speaks words that otherwise demean your very good body:

1. *Consider the source.* Is the person who is refuting the truth that our bodies are not markers of our righteousness

someone we can trust? Do they see God and the kingdom and His Word in the same light that we do? Do they use the Word as a weapon against people or as a weapon against the enemy? Do they search and seek the Word humbly in order to know God better or to *seem* as if they know God better? Are they willing to be wrong and thus be redirected? Do they seek to honor God with their own body? Do they have a kingdom-minded mentality toward their own body?

Only you can answer these questions, but I will tell you this as plainly as possible: you can love and respect and honor someone, yet choose not to accept their perspective if you do not believe their beliefs about the body align with the heart of God. You can perhaps learn from them about other things, but push the mute button in your soul when they talk about the body.

I believe humility says I can learn from anyone about anything. But in an area of my life as fragile and as precious as the way I perceive my body, where I have experienced extreme hurt and miraculous healing, I do not consent to be taught by people who do not have a kingdom-minded mentality.

2. *Only you can know in your heart what it means for you to "take care of your body."* Again, we can be humble and learn from others here, but the benchmarks are too disparate and too often based on the opinions of other humans, who (surprise!) may not have a kingdom-minded mentality about the body. Is taking care of your body resting it, moving it, eating healthy meals? Or is "taking care of your body" a euphemism for pushing it hard toward cultural ideals? Is taking care of your body being on a specialized diet? Is taking care of your body utilizing homeopathic remedies?

I have friends who take care of their bodies and run marathons. I have friends who take care of their bodies and may not be able to run a mile if they tried. I have friends who take care of their bodies by eating very intentional things at intentional times, and I have friends who take care of their bodies by embracing freedom in what they eat. I have friends who take care of their bodies and get copious facials and friends who take care of their bodies and would never put a foreign chemical in or on their skin.

If we're going to send up a loud, firm rebuttal to the idea that our righteousness is determined by the state of our bodies, we need to know what taking care of our bodies means for us and not what other people think it should mean. Of course we should take care of our bodies, and of course we should not believe that this will look the same for everyone. However, we must go to God ourselves and ask Him what it looks like for us to take care of our bodies.

3. *Remember that not everyone is on the same page.* To have a meaningful conversation with anyone who wants to discuss the connection between righteousness and how we treat our bodies, I suggest we start from the same premise, which is often difficult. We can't discuss potential rebuttals unless we're standing on the same firm ground of truth. For me, that truth is that God made our bodies good, and any way I treat my body is a response to that goodness rather than a punishment of my body for being bad.

This may seem like it should be understood, but I find that it is not. Instead, the general assumption seems to be that we must work *for the approval* of God and others with our bodies rather than work *from the approval* of God. Simply put, I believe many followers of Jesus are trying to make their bodies good, rather than agreeing that God already made them good and treating them as such.

*So shouldn't you take care of your body to honor God?* Absolutely.

*Do we agree about what that means and what it will look like?* I'd say it's almost impossible for us to all work from the same premise or perspective, because we all have different bodies with unique needs.

*Does that mean my body is an indicator of righteousness, of whether or not I'm fit to step into His calling on my life?* Absolutely not. God looks at the heart.

We should, too.

## Put It into Practice

Let's maintain our rhythm of not just retaining knowledge but putting truth into action.

### First, some hard questions:

1. *Have you believed, agreed, and/or shared the message that our bodies are markers of our righteousness?*

   What made you say that in the past? What impact did that have on you?

2. *How does it make you feel to remember that God looks at the heart?*

   Does this lead you back to worship or, perhaps, to worry that you've neglected the most important part of yourself? What do you perceive He sees when He looks at your heart?

3. *Have you felt disqualified because of your body?*

   What would it look like for you to throw that off today and step into the calling God has given you?

**Now, let's try some life-giving practices:**

1. *This week, try eating as an act of worship.* What if eating wasn't about punishment or pleasure apart from God? What if it wasn't about withholding or seeking comfort? What if it was about thanking God for His good gifts and nourishing your body for the work He's set before you?

   > So whether you eat or drink or whatever you do, do it all for the glory of God. (1 Cor. 10:31)

2. *This week, try movement/exercise as an act of worship.* What if moving wasn't about fixing your body or provoking it or treating it as a project? What if moving was about taking care of the vessel He's placed you in and using those moments to praise Him, thank Him, and glorify Him with what you've got?

   I'm often asked how to worship when you exercise if you hate exercise, and I think the simplest answer is to find some way to move that you don't hate! Go on a walk with a friend and talk about your hearts—that's worship. Throw on music you love and move your body in private—that's worship. Go to the prettiest place in your city and walk and wonder at the goodness of God—that's worship.

3. *Spend time digging into God's Word in order to understand what* does *make you righteous and holy before God.* Again, we're going to replace lies with truth so we can see our perspectives of our body restored and our minds renewed.

   Check out 2 Corinthians 5:21, Romans 10:4, 1 Peter 2:24, and Romans 3:22–24.

# Words from Our Friends

**Jensine:** *What a reminder of what God looks at (the heart, the heart, the heart!). It makes me remember all the faithful people in the Bible—not much is made of their bulging biceps or flat stomachs. The most physical we get is when we're talking the about the way we get to enjoy the good, good gift of marriage! But what we do get in God's Word are glimpses of faithfulness over and over, of trusting in the goodness of God to bring the fruit.*

**Sarah:** *As a home health physical therapist, I work with a lot of older adults. Throughout the years, I've worked with many older women in their nineties who were still defining themselves by the way they look. These women accomplished amazing things in their lives, but they continuously spoke about themselves in discouraging terms, all relating to their bodies. Working with these women was a wake-up call for me. I realized I don't want to be ninety and still struggling with disordered eating or defining my worth in terms of my body. I want to be defined by simply being the woman God made me to be, by my faith- fulness, and by the way that I love others. I'm so thankful the Lord looks at the heart and that my body doesn't define me. Now, when I work with these patients, I remind them, "Don't talk about my friend like that," and spend some time affirming their bodies for what they can do, not what they look like.*

CHAPTER 9

# Welcoming Revival

My husband always says, "Questions mean you care." We say it a lot in the context of our church. If you have questions about something we've done or said or something we're going to do or say, it's so much more helpful to ask a question than to make an assumption. A question is a loving act that demonstrates your investment. For us, questions aren't about mistrust or doubt; they're about honest engagement and creating a solid foundation from which to grow. This is partially why I've asked you so many in-depth and soul-baring questions in the previous chapters.

Let's revisit a few of those, a quick greatest hits tour, if you will:

What have you been told about your body and the source of its worth?

What does it look like for the kingdom to come in your
body today?
Do you feel like you've been trying to beat the curse as it
pertains to your body?
What's the truest thing about you?
Why do you want healing and restoration in your body?

If you've answered these questions, I pray it hasn't been with rote responses, but rather an exploration that has led you to see yourself, God, and this world more clearly. If you've answered these questions, I pray they've left you not just exposed but expectant. I pray these questions have sparked growth and change in your soul. I pray they've produced godly fruit that lasts.

Good questions clue us into where we're at and give us insight about where we think we're going. When I coach women, in mission or in business or in anything else, I often start with three questions:

How are you feeling today?
How willing are you to change and grow?
What will happen if you don't experience growth in
this area?

This feels like a pertinent and productive place for us to pause and ask those questions regarding our body image, but in addition, I've got one more important question for us to dig into.

When I first started writing this book, I sent a quick survey to a few friends around the world. I asked them about their varying views regarding their bodies, their experiences, their pain points, and their hopes. But I ended the survey with the one question whose answer feels most important:

"On a scale of 1 to 5, how likely is it that our generation

can experience breakthrough in the stronghold of negative body image?"

I'm delighted to tell you that 70 percent of my friends answered "5"—very hopeful, and the other 30 percent answered 4.

How we answer this question doesn't just unveil something important about our hearts; how we answer this question also points to how we'll live out the truth that our bodies are good. This is worth mulling over. If we don't believe we can experience healing collectively, we won't move forward in trying to be healed.

Revival is an incredibly important part of the path for those of us who are on our way to agreeing that our bodies are good. Why is it important?

There are two areas of revival I'm interested in: personal revival and collective revival. Here's why:

First, on this path to believing our bodies are good, we rename what the world has maligned in order to return to what God has said about us from the beginning. We gather the grace that's been offered to us and discard the negative words that have been spoken over our bodies. We pick up the first name given to us by God: *good*. We live into that name, we shake our heads *yes*, and we agree with it.

Second, we give our bodies rest by declaring that they are good—they're not on a path to becoming better or acceptable because they were already made good. We learn that we can move our bodies and take care of them in love, without provocation, without treating them like projects to finish or problems to fix.

Third, we experience restoration. We remember what our bodies are for: worship. Worship is the space in which we experience God, encounter His goodness, and remember some of the best news about our bodies—that we won't experience them in this fallen state forever. But in the meantime, we seek to understand what it looks like to be in awe of God in our bodies.

We could stop there. And even if we did, we would notice some positive changes in our own lives. Or, once we've internalized this message for ourselves, we can speak it out, using this same truth and language to love the women around us. We can keep it to ourselves, or we can witness a collective healing, the restoration and renewal of a generation. We can have partners to run forward with into restoration, and there will be no turning back.

I think we want both: personal revival *and* collective revival. We don't want to settle for just having a new set of ideas. We want to be fully changed, and we want to bring our sisters along for the ride.

## Do You Want Revival?

When we see results, we want to keep going. If we don't see results, we'll lose hope and lose heart and quit. This is a kingdom principle.

> Hope deferred makes the heart sick,
> but a longing fulfilled is a tree of life. (Prov. 13:12)

Here's what I know about you, kingdom women. You want good for yourselves, but you also intrinsically want good for others. You want to experience the freedom that was purchased for you on the cross of Christ, but you'll dance with joy and run with exuberance when you see other women step into that freedom. You want evidence of transformation for yourself, but you long to see the same transformation in other people. And that's beautiful.

Here's something else I know about you, kingdom women. At the end of the day, you know that if there is any hope to be had, it's in the power of Jesus Christ, who rose from the dead and resurrected our souls. At the very core of who you are, you may trust general wisdom and knowledge, but you'll lean the full weight of your life and eternity on Him and His truth. You love people, and you love learning, but you worship Jesus. Whether or not you picked up this book believing that God is the answer, you know in your heart of hearts that His healing is our best hope. You trust God, even when you can't see how He'll show up.

And here's what I know about our Father: He doesn't leave us or forsake us. He doesn't want His daughters to linger in bondage forever. He grows us; He allows us to grow from generation to generation. He's a way maker. He's a culture shifter. He's the ultimate healer. He's the rebuilder of ancient ruins, the one who wipes every tear from every eye. He is behind every beautiful cultural advance and every kingdom initiative. I know that I know that I know that He wants us to see liberation in our lifetimes. I know that He wants the women who come behind us to step into more freedom than we can imagine. And I know that when we ask Him for bread, He won't give us a stone.

The variable is not God and His capacity, but *us*. The question isn't, "Can God do it?" but "Will we be there for the breakthrough when revival happens? Will we declare that freedom is ours for the taking? Will we see the first fruits of liberty as the women around us take hold of what has been taken hold of for them? Will we look for the results and keep pressing in to see more?"

The most important question you and I may have to answer is this: Do we want to be a part of the revival that will take place when the women of our generation begin to believe their bodies are good and start acting like they do?

Can you imagine if women no longer sized each other up

before stepping on the treadmill at the gym? If you could look in the mirror, exhale with ease, and see what God sees? If your daughter didn't feel pressed to count calories like her friends at school? Can you imagine us all walking and moving in freedom, no matter the season, in bathing suits or sweat suits? What if our granddaughters and their daughters intrinsically believed their bodies were good, made and loved by God, and they loved their bodies well rather than trying to make themselves lovable?

Will we stick around and be on the front lines when change starts to happen? Will we be expectantly waiting and praying when shackles start clanging to the ground and women start reveling in the good news that they're loved and treasured just because God made them? Will we be marching with them when the momentum builds and it's time to harvest the seeds of truth that we've planted?

Hope deferred makes a heart sick, but when our Savior is involved, there's always movement and promise and HOPE. So there's no chance we'll miss out on seeing the first fruits—unless we give up before it's harvest time.

## How Revival Starts

Have you ever watched *The Office*? If you did, you're about to giggle. If you didn't, you're going to want to google this scene when you're done reading, and then you'll giggle. There is a scene when Michael, the main character, who is a lovable buffoon, realizes he may have to declare bankruptcy. He's kind of like an overgrown child who is completely unaware of what's happening around him socially, so it's not a huge surprise that his finances are a mess.

In this episode, Creed (who is perhaps one of the strangest characters) advises Michael to declare bankruptcy. So Michael walks into the middle of the office and solemnly yells:

"I . . . DECLARE . . . BANKRUPTCYYYYYYY."

Of course, that's not how it works. But this is kind of how I see people treating revival in the church. You can't just say the word "revival" and suddenly see throngs of people returning to God. You can't stir up a revival just by declaring it so—that's God's job. My husband, who is also my pastor, sometimes reminds me that often, we don't know something is a revival until after it's happened. And when you're caught up in a revival, I imagine you're too enraptured by the power and presence of God to go around telling people you're experiencing revival, claiming you caused it or called it into being.

I sense that when we see true revival, we'll be so in awe of God, we won't want to lay claim to our part in it. We'll be hesitant to take credit for it, or even to trace the path back to its origin. We'll simply experience revival and that will be enough.

So what *does* usher in revival, the unprecedented movements of God that rewrite history and change the shape of God's family for eternity?

Let's look together.

> "If my people, who are called by my name, will humble them-
> selves and pray and seek my face and turn from their wicked
> ways, then I will hear from heaven, and I will forgive their sin
> and will heal their land." (2 Chron. 7:14)

Let's start with The Great Awakening of 1727. It was notable because there was a discernible outpouring of the Spirit of God across different continents. No Instagram. No worship on iTunes. No large gathering. Just massive numbers of people coming to know God, at one time, in Germany, England, and America. It's estimated that more than 30,000 people came to believe in Jesus and at least 150 new churches were established. Again—no internet. No Zoom calls where people could share the fruit they were seeing. And this revival's roots? *The entire awakening is traced to an extended period of prayer, repentance, and reconciliation that began in a small Moravian community in Germany.*

Let's move on to Charles Finney. My husband and I are both Finney fans, reading everything we can get our hands on and paying close attention to his ministry. Charles Finney was at the forefront of the Second Great Awakening that took place around 1830. It's estimated that over 100,000 people dedicated their lives to Jesus in the span of one year in North America, and the effects of the revival were felt in England and all over Europe. Charles Finney, who was an attorney by trade, met Jesus when he went out into the woods to settle the account of his soul once and for all. Afterward, he recounted that the Holy Spirit "seemed to go through me . . . body and soul."

He was infamous for his calls to repentance, even known for making his sermons "less pleasing and more productive." Finney believed that to speak frankly about sin, hell, grace, redemption, and salvation was the most loving thing you could do for someone who gave you their attention. All those calls to repentance led to revival.

From studying revivals from around the world, I surmise that they can't be manufactured, and they can't be stopped, and they are more often than not preceded by repentance, prayer, and a desire to see God do what only God can do.

My hope for this chapter is not that you hear me declaring revival, because I'm pretty sure I'd sound a lot like Michael Scott. But I do pray we can catch a whiff of the aroma of possibility that whirls around us as women of God. I pray we perceive the power of God as available to us, to transform our own lives, and to catapult our current culture and generation into a space of healing like we've never seen before. And I pray we will pause for a moment to count the cost of what would keep us from being a part of the renewal God may bring pertaining to how women see their bodies.

## Revival Means Moving Forward, Not Turning Back

It is for freedom that Christ has set us free. Stand firm, then, and do not let yourselves be burdened again by a yoke of slavery. (Gal. 5:1)

The first book I had the joy of writing, *Wild and Free*, was coauthored with my dear friend, Hayley Morgan. We switched off writing chapters—I wrote the chapters on being "wild" (getting back to our true nature as daughters of God), and Hayley wrote the chapters on being "free" (acting in the liberty that is ours in Christ Jesus). I'm grieved, but not embarrassed, to share with you that I'd often tell Hayley in private that there was no way I could write about freedom, specifically because I felt like I was in bondage regarding my body. My chains were breaking, but I was still struggling.

Hayley wrote a lot about Harriet Tubman and her relentless pursuit to see the freedom of other Black people who were enslaved in America. She wrote about how Harriet tasted freedom and had to have it for others, so she repeatedly put herself in the path of bodily harm to ensure others would be rescued. It wasn't until a few years later that I found out about the famous photograph of Harriet Tubman holding a shotgun. Harriet was known to carry a firearm in order to defend herself and other people escaping slavery, but she also admitted to turning the gun on those who tried to go back, as a means to keep them moving forward.

If a person who was escaping slavery turned back in fear, he or she caused extreme peril for those who'd helped them escape and for those who had found freedom. They couldn't afford to allow backtracking.

The stakes are different for women today who are seeking freedom from the belief that their bodies aren't good enough. But the danger of backtracking remains. When a woman returns to her old, familiar bondage, it puts those who are free and those who have led them to freedom at risk.

Maybe this book should have come with a really gentle warning label: DON'T READ THIS BOOK UNLESS YOU'RE WILLING TO STAY OUTSIDE THE CULTURAL CONFINES AND EXPECTATIONS. Except I know the book doesn't make our bondage any more dangerous—it's always been important that we fight for freedom, not just for ourselves, but for those around us.

Women are watching you. Your daughters, sisters, mother are watching you. The gal who babysits for you, the one who sits two rows behind you at church, the other students in your school. Your roommate, your barista, the gals in your exercise class. They are all up against the same fight, the same struggle, whether they know it or not. The enemy of their souls is waging the same war against their bodies and their understanding of their worth. And that's not to say it's all up to you, or that you have to be the hero. Jesus is the hero! He's got them. He loves them. He has a plan for their redemption. But you can be a part of His plan.

We all get to choose whether we'll play a part in the journeys of the women around us as they come to see their bodies in a kingdom light or whether we'll contribute to the cultural soundtrack that is keeping them in bondage. We all get to decide, with every conversation, with every worshipful move we make with our own bodies, if we'll be a spark of light in a dark place.

We all get to decide which side we want to be on if revival hits and women across the world begin to throw off the bondage that has held them captive to the expectations of this world.

But it's good for us to remember that the revival won't start around a table in a boardroom. It won't start with a slogan or a slickly marketed campaign. It won't begin rolling forward when we sing the right songs or wear the cute T-shirts or even when we walk to the middle of the room and yell, "I DECLARE REVIVAL!" If and when revival comes, and this story begins to shift for the women in our time, it will be because the daughters of God repented, prayed, and decided they wanted to see their Father in a clearer light than they did before. It may be quiet, and it will probably be messy, but it can begin today.

## Revival Is Stirred by Repentance

In my family, I'm known for apologizing. This is for two reasons: (a) I sin a lot, and (b) I care about apologizing. It can be hard for my people to handle because I can be a pain about *how* people say they're sorry. For example, in our home, if you say you're sorry, you're likely to hear a follow-up question: "For what?" I want my kids to be able to express what they did wrong, why they're sorry, and how they'll correct the behavior in the future. I try not to be a pain about it, but I think how you apologize matters.

For example, I hate the phrase, "I'm sorry if that hurt your feelings—that wasn't my intention." Maybe it wasn't our intention, but don't you think we say this far too often when we don't actually mean it? Don't you agree that sometimes, we *do* mean to hurt the other person, but it's not culturally appropriate to say so? And don't you think we'd experience more restoration if we were able to identify our sin more clearly, say we're sorry, experience grace, and then be compelled by grace to not engage in that sin again? I think we often find ourselves in rhythms and patterns of perpetual sin because we just can't identify what we've done with clarity, or we try to clean it up and make it sound less bad.

I personally love repenting. I love telling God I'm sorry because He never fails to forgive, and when I air all my mistakes and mess-ups, it's incredibly freeing. I still find myself avoiding it at times, when pride feels like the pacifier that will keep my ego safe. But at this point in the game, my soul often wins out over my flesh and sends me back to the feet of Jesus to say I'm sorry. I love the refreshment that comes from repentance—and it's not just a human principle; it's one that is established in the kingdom:

> "Repent, then, and turn to God, so that your sins may be wiped out, that times of refreshing may come from the Lord." (Acts 3:19)

Repentance will be important in any revival the women in our culture experience because historically , we see evidence of that pattern. But, we also can't expect to see revival if we don't start with repentance, because without truly contrite hearts, we're much more likely to return to the captivity of our culture. If we don't pause and tell God we're sorry for how we haven't lived and believed as if our bodies are good, we won't experience the refreshment that will keep our souls pressing forward. And if we simply try to modify our behavior instead of surrendering our hearts, we won't see the kind of true and lasting fruit that will motivate us to keep going.

The word for repent in Acts 3:19 is μετανοέω or *metanoeó*, which means to turn, to change your mind, to think differently afterward. We've talked about how we're subject to believe and receive what we're told when we're young. But that's not the case now that we're grown up. We have an opportunity to pledge our allegiance to the kingdom and adopt a belief system about our bodies that is rooted in truth, beauty, and agreement with what God says about us.

Now we've had our eyes opened to the very good news that God says our body is good. We've acknowledged that we have the capacity to agree with that truth by renaming our bodies and the bodies around us as good. We know we can rest our bodies, not just physically, but in a deep and spiritual way, by ceasing to provoke our bodies and treating them like a project. We can experience Jesus through restoration, using our bodies not as an afterthought, but as the space where we worship and bring Him glory. And! And! And! Because there is so much brokenness pertaining to how women view their bodies, this firm ground of body image can be a space where we see revival come in our culture, in the women of our generation, no matter what age we are.

Many of us have moved from seeing our bodies as the enemy or the most broken place in our lives to seeing them as fertile ground where fruit is growing. We've moved from seeing our bodies as our greatest weakness to seeing them as the area where we have the most potential power, where His strength is shining in the dark.

But will we stay here? Will we change our minds? Will we share this message? Will we move forward and keep repenting? Or will we turn back to the bondage we've always known?

## Glory Keeps Me Going

If we want to see a tsunami of revival pertaining to how the daughters of God see their bodies, we need to start with repentance.

Nothing will teach you repentance like having a daughter who is watching your every move.

My daughter Gloriana's birth and arrival, her very presence, has constantly caused me to ask myself hard questions: *What will she hear me say about my body? What is she learning from me? What is she picking up on?* But if you ask anyone who knows her, they'll confirm that she's a leader. She's been shifting the culture around her since she was born. And while I know she is watching me and listening to me, I'm also watching her and listening to her, and learning while I'm at it.

It's hard to say if my determination not to talk about my body in a negative way rubbed off on Glory or if she was always just going to love her body. I do know that during some of her formative years, God was bringing healing into my life, and it was bearing fruit. I was running marathons and wearing high-waisted jeans and refusing to use the term "baby weight," when the culture said I should have been counting calories and hiding my body. When most women my age were vowing to put on a one-piece and keep their stretch marks hidden, I was deciding that my body is my body and there's no use trying to hide it anymore. I'm not wearing thong bikinis or anything, but I'm also not waiting until I have a six-pack to put on a two-piece, you know?

I was asking myself hard questions, like, *What will she hear you say about your body?* And amazingly, I was seeing the fruit—*in her.* Glory has loved her body and loved how God made her since she could really perceive it. She delights in the way she mirrors Him, she smiles at her own reflection, she laughs off her "imperfections." I'd catch her, as young as eight years old, seeing a glimpse of herself in the mirror and smiling with delight. She's not self-centered or prideful about her looks, but she loves who God made her to be. She should. She's a miraculous work of art. And I mean that with all I've got.

As I worked to model the kind of self-image I hoped my daughter would have, I was seeing the fruit in this little woman who was growing up in my house. And her ferocious freedom led me to want to stay in my own freedom. I didn't want to undo the incredible work of God, to begin moving backward or picking up limitations that He never placed on me. Glory makes me want to keep inching forward, finding more liberty and grace and belief in His goodness with every step.

But because life keeps happening and the culture continues to be loud and in my face, I have to keep repenting. I have to keep telling God I'm sorry. He keeps showing me areas where I value what the world tells me over what He's said. The Holy Spirit, in love and gentleness, clues me in to selfish motivations or desires for approval that are swirling just beneath the surface of my soul. I have to pause, expose my heart to the light of God's love and truth, and turn back to Him once again.

I guess you could say that in my little home and in my heart, I've experienced revival. I've moved from practicing multiple forms of disordered eating to the freedom to listen to God when I'm hungry and about what I want to eat. I've gone from hating my body to genuinely appreciating the way God made it. I've gone from using clothing as a mask to hide what I don't love to picking what I wear with intention because color and decoration feel like a way to worshipfully light up my world. I move my body, not as punishment but as praise—as an exploration of what He's made me able to do. I rest when I need to, because I know God gives rest to those He loves.

It's taken years of heart work (not necessarily steps or programs, which is why I've been so hesitant to give you any), years of wrestling over this statement until I believe it with all that I've got: *my body is good*.

But I have seen revival. I have seen the deadest and most decaying part of my life become one of the most fruitful. I have seen color return. I have seen healing. I have felt loved by God. He has awakened my desire to share this message and to see as many women walk in freedom as humanly possible. All I want to do is invite you to join me in sharing it.

I love you too much to ask you to partner in something that's impossible. But God and Glory have shown me that revival is real—it's on the table, it's attainable—if we'll keep asking the hard questions, keep seeking to see the fruit in the lives of other women, keep running to freedom and away from bondage, and keep repenting when we need to.

Revival is waiting.

## Questions

If repentance, prayer, and returning are how revival begins, are you in?

Are you on the lookout for other women walking in freedom? What happens when you see this kind of fruit?

How likely is it, in your opinion, that women in our time and culture can see breakthrough in the stronghold of negative body image?

When was the last time you told God you're sorry for how you've treated your body?

# Words from Our Friends

**Kim:** *Let's goooo! I'm so here for this. I'm ready to understand and experience what it looks like to be "in awe of God in my body." I desperately want to be a part of this revival for myself, for my daughters, and for the women of this generation. I'm going to get really honest and confess that I have never repented for how I've treated my body. It's not because I was knowingly being rebellious, but simply because I didn't realize this was an area of my life that I was withholding from Jesus. I thank God for this revelation! I'm coming to Him with a surrendered heart and allowing Him to illuminate this area of my life that has been hidden for far too long. I'm going to begin looking for freedom and revival in myself and other women. I want to champion other women, and that starts with me. Revival in my own heart, in this area of my life, starts with repentance and running to freedom. I'm not going to miss out on this!*

CHAPTER 10

# Your Body Is Not a Trophy

Trophies are funny things. We're supposed to feel a personal sense of achievement because of some fake gold plastic thingamajig purchased from an online catalog? Note that my distinct lack of trophies has probably given me this perspective. So if you've got a million trophies, and you see this differently, grace and peace to you.

I was around nine years old when I joined the Capital Textiles T-ball team. I remember the first practice and parents' meeting. I remember the way the coach looked exactly like a Little League coach you'd see on TV. I remember being the only girl, and I remember not necessarily loving the idea of playing T-ball. I can't remember if I explicitly complained about having to go or just sucked it up, but I know my mom was just trying to love me well by enrolling me to play, so I think I probably surmised that and just went with the flow.

I was really, really bad at T-ball. And the boys on my team actually seemed to care about winning, which I couldn't quite grasp, so I was pretty obnoxious to them. But there was a bright side. By about halfway through the season, they had a nickname for me, and I *loved* it: *Lightning*. Because I was so fast, of course. I tried to live into that nickname—I promise you, there were times when I must have been a blur running around those bases because I was going so fast. I even asked my teammates, "Could you guys even see me? I was going so fast!"

They put the name "Lightning" on my trophy, and I admit I took it a little too far. I got lightning bolt stickers for my notebook at school, got lightning bolt dangly earrings to wear, and I even entertained getting a little lightning bolt shaved into my early-90s undercut boy haircut, but somebody smart stopped me.

At some point, I was informed that they had nicknamed me *Lightning* because I was so *slow*.

I threw the trophy away.

I'm bitter about trophies, OK? They're not my favorite thing.

Trophies aren't necessarily the best thing for those of us who are kingdom-minded and living with an eternal focus. It seems like trophies keep us believing that the best thing we can do is rack up approval on earth, even though it's the approval of our Father that means the most. It seems as though trophies are images that give *us* glory, rather than putting it where it belongs—at the feet of Jesus.

I'm not saying we should burn all our trophies, but maybe it's worthwhile to consider why we seek them, why we keep them, and maybe even ask ourselves, *Are we holding these symbols in too much esteem? Are we putting too much stock in them?*

First, let's not believe for even a second that our obsession with awards and accolades ended after Little League. We all long to receive our own version of recognition. Here are a few desires for recognition that seem to prevail among those of us who have passed elementary school:

We want to get on the dean's list.
We want to get scholarships.
We want to get recognized at the meeting.
We long to be thanked publicly.
We wish we could win the Yard of the Month award.
We'd love to see our picture in the newsletter.
It would be cool if the pastor would mention us from the pulpit.
We want to be thanked at the back of the book.
We want someone to call us their best friend.
We wish they would tag us in that post.
I want the book to get the award.
We want to get verified on Instagram.
We measure our credit financially.

And we treat our bodies like the ultimate trophy.

Telling a friend she's lost weight has somehow become the ultimate compliment. When we grow past the cultural absurdity of commenting on people's literal weight, we find other ways to notice and notarize one another for how we look. This practice isn't found only outside of Christian culture; instead, this is just one measurement of the world we've completely co-opted. We've even added spiritual weight to support it, whether intentionally or unintentionally.

We celebrate when a friend "bounces back" quickly after a baby, we glorify the "glow up" (a season when a tween or teen goes from looking awkward to awesome by the world's standards), we praise one another when we eat less and call it "self control." In short, we tend to turn something God never ordained into something spiritual.

We treat our bodies like trophies, statues representing what we idolize: the approval and attention of others. This is problematic first and foremost because that glory belongs to God.

What if the final straw, the thing that will tip the scales toward revival, is the counter-cultural decision that any distinction or honor we're given gets laid at the feet of Jesus? What if we decide that any trophy or award we receive will be relinquished so we become less concerned with how many accolades we can garner, and instead, use our energy to worship Jesus? What if revival comes in our communities because we break the matrix and scream at the enemy, "Making our bodies better was never necessary! They were made good!"

What if revival comes because we decide our bodies are not trophies to begin with?

## Why the Trophies Have to Burn

The women in my family, gals of the New South that we are, have a few phrases that are so Southern and saccharine they'll make your teeth hurt. But they're hard to quit.

"More jewels in your crown!" we shout when we see each other doing something holy, something virtuous, something often unseen. When you're kind to the fussy lady at church who always tries to be secretly spiteful to you, it's "More jewels in your crown!" When you watch your sister's kids even though you're having a really full and hard work week, it's "More jewels in your crown!" When you're caught cleaning up the mess someone else made, it's "More jewels in your crown!"

I say it to my sisters because I know they get the gospel, the truth that Jesus is enough when they aren't. I say it to them because I know they don't believe they can earn their way into heaven, and because the idea of a heavenly crown is rooted in Scripture.

James 1 and Revelation 2 speak to the "crown of life" that will be given to those who suffer and persevere under trials. The "incorruptible crown" is also referenced in 1 Corinthians 9 and will be bestowed on those who demonstrate self-denial and perseverance. Second Timothy 4 speaks of a "crown of righteousness" for those who anticipate the second coming of Jesus, and there's a "crown of glory" for those who minister and preach the gospel in 1 Peter 5. My favorite, the "crown of rejoicing," shows up in 1 Thessalonians 2, for those who engage in evangelism outside the Christian church. If you've ever known an evangelist, someone who is passionate about seeing other people walk with Jesus, I bet you can picture them rejoicing a *ton* in heaven.

Then, there's the passage in Revelation that describes what will happen as the elders lay their crowns at the feet of Jesus:

> Whenever the living creatures give glory, honor and thanks to him who sits on the throne and who lives for ever and ever, the twenty-four elders fall down before him who sits on the throne and worship him who lives for ever and ever. They lay their crowns before the throne and say:
>
> > "You are worthy, our Lord and God;
> > > to receive glory and honor and power,
> > for you created all things,
> > > and by your will they were created
> > > and have their being." (Rev. 4:9–11)

Scripture speaks of a heavenly reward for eternal work, but even then, it makes it clear that we'll be compelled to send these trophies and rewards right back to the throne. Whatever jewels are in your crown, I know you'll count them as nothing when you encounter the grace and glory of God. Whatever trophies come our way, we'll gladly reroute them to Him, because He deserves them.

But make no mistake! These trophies, these crowns, these jewels, these gifts of glittering glory are about *eternal work* and are of *eternal worth*. They are not our bodies. Our bodies are not trophies. Our bodies are temples of the Holy Spirit, the home of our heaven-bound souls. It is a trick, a tool, a tactic of the enemy of our souls to make us believe that our bodies' worth is in any way determined by human opinion or perception.

Your body is not the crown you're going to lay at the feet of Jesus. Your beauty is not the jewel you're going to give back to Him. Your body is good because He made it, but it's not the most important thing about you. Your body can't be the best thing about you, namely because you are so much *more* than your body. And we will all see healing, restoration, and revival when we decide to stop agreeing with any idea that promotes such thinking.

## So What Do You Say

There's something funny about playing devil's advocate. We play devil's advocate when we support the opposing side of an argument, just to highlight the potential merit of an opposing idea. It's one of those phrases we've simply accepted as part of our cultural language, and sometimes we're even seen as mature and thoughtful when we play this role or allow someone else to do so.

But when it comes to the word God has spoken over your body, do you really want to advocate for the devil? Do you want to spend even a moment of your precious life fighting for his cause? OK, so maybe we don't always know where the line is between good and evil in every argument. Maybe some things are gray areas, worth measuring and sorting out from all sides. But is this one of those moments? Let's revisit what we know to be true.

God made our bodies good (Gen. 1:31). Our enemy (the devil) tempted humans with the intent to allow sin to enter our world, and thus, cause us to experience brokenness in these good bodies (Gen. 3:1–7).

Personally, I'm not super tempted to be his advocate in this area.

God cares what happens to our bodies (Matt. 6:30). He does not want us to experience pain, harm, or brokenness. The enemy comes to kill, steal, and destroy our bodies. He uses sickness, abuse, the environment, the sin of others, and the decay of earth to do just that (John 10:10).

Still not really wanting to be on his team here. You?

God values women, the *whole* of who they are, and their place in His kingdom. Satan (our enemy, the devil) perpetuates a campaign against women that causes them to be devalued, objectified, and continually condemned by the measurement of beauty that is perceived and determined by the world. This leads to negative body image, disordered eating, trauma, mistreatment of our bodies, and a host of other horrific issues.

So you might be asking, "Does this mean you're not proud of your body? Does this mean you don't enjoy it when you look pretty? Does this mean you don't wear makeup?"

Nah, girl! I love my body. It's good. I love celebrating how God made it and giving Him glory with it. When a friend tells me I look beautiful, I slap a smile on my face and say, "Thank you!" I don't argue or tell her ten reasons why she's wrong. I thank God that he made us all so interesting and distinct, and I praise Him for the ways He created me unique. I celebrate when my body grows in strength and can do something new. I do handstands and run marathons and jump on the trampoline with my kids. But I work hard not to lose heart when my body can't do something, too—like the splits, or jumping on the trampoline without peeing my pants. (Gals in your twenties and younger, you don't know about this yet—it happens).

Here's some of the ways I've learned to respond to comments about my body, whether they're echoing God's good truth or perhaps playing a little devil's advocate:

**You look beautiful!**
  *My response:* "Thank you!"
**You look like you've lost weight!**
  *My response:* "Oh yeah? That's interesting." (I make a face to show them this is not a conversation I'm willing to have with them.)
    *What I mean is, "I think it's interesting that you use weight as a defining characteristic of value and beauty." If they dig further, continue to comment, I'll even open up that discussion. Should I just be polite and say thank you? I believe, no.*
**Have you been doing something different?**
  *My response:* If I have, I'll tell them. If I haven't, a simple no will suffice.
**You look thin today!**
  *My response:* "Interesting. I hope I look like me! I love looking like me."

I find that it helps to have my responses planned, so I'm not put on the spot. I trust you'll find language that feels true to you, but I entreat you to remember two things as your body becomes the subject of conversation:

1. *Keeping the status quo will keep the status quo.* If you let your concern about being awkward or saying something out of the ordinary inform your decisions, it will. If you choose politeness as a tactic to avoid conflict when something unjust is said, you'll keep the status quo but potentially miss an opportunity for growth.

2. *Playing nice is not the strategy that will win against spiritual strongholds.* Second Corinthians 10 tells us to take captive every idea that puts itself up against the knowledge of God. I don't need to treat sin politely, and I am not obligated to respond to bondage sweetly. I don't need to be rude, but I will not be taken back into captivity for the sake of other people's feelings.

> We demolish arguments and every pretension that
> sets itself up against the knowledge of God, and we
> take captive every thought to make it obedient to
> Christ. (2 Cor. 10:5)

We won't see revival unless we repent and relinquish the idea that our bodies are trophies, or that they're up for consideration or scrutiny by our culture, or by every individual we encounter.

Here's my gift to you: when the conversations get too awkward, you can always hand them your own well-worn copy of this book. I can take the heat for you.

Your body is not the world's to weigh in on. Your body is not a project or a marker of righteousness. Your body is neither a trophy nor the best thing about you.

If by grace, through faith, you are a follower of Jesus, you are a daughter of the Most High God. You were made with intention and creativity, celebration and excellence. Your body was made and pronounced good by the ultimate Creator, Judge, Savior, and Hero of the world. He mourns the mess of sin and brokenness that we live in, but He doesn't leave us—He brings redemption and restoration to these bodies of ours. And He promises us a day when our earthly shells will be a distant memory, a shadow, a vapor that used to be.

Your body is good. The world is wrong. The enemy is a liar. Rest and restoration and revival are yours for the taking. Let's get after it.

# Put It into Practice

Let's keep our rhythm of not just retaining knowledge, but putting truth into action.

**First, some hard questions:**

1. *Do you want revival?*

   As it pertains to women's bodies and their worth, would you rather things stay the same? Do you enjoy the status quo? Do you benefit from it? What do you stand to lose if women begin to believe their bodies are good?

2. *Do you know what's good about you?*

   If we no longer measure our worth by how much others approve of our bodies, can you readily access where your value lies?

3. *Are you ready to be a little awkward in order to fight the strongholds of negative body image?*

   The question behind this question is, "Do we value being seen as normal more than we value following Jesus? Do we value being accepted more than we want freedom for those around us?"

**Now, let's try some life-giving practices:**

1. *Pay attention to how you give compliments.* Be cautious and careful about how you give praise. Try encouraging others with phrases and words that don't align with the world's perception of how women should be.

   Tell your friends they look strong.

   Tell them you're proud of how obedient they are.

   Compliment them when they use their spiritual gifts.

   Tell them they look radiant, alive, exciting, or abundant.

   Better yet, tell them everything that's amazing about them that has nothing to do with their bodies.

2. *Pay attention to how you receive compliments or comments about your body.* When people say negative things, practice ambivalence and/or redirecting them. Don't be scared to stay neutral or even reject what feels like it's not from God.

3. *Think about your trophies.* What trappings of this world do you rely on as sources of your worth? Let's not stop at our bodies; let's keep going until we remember where our true worth and value comes from. Let's see revival in all the places, amen?

# CHAPTER 11

# Freedom Starts Today

I love a good timeline. I love to trace God's movements through dates and chronological concrete moments of His grace being poured out.

Recently, for the wedding of one of my best friends, I gave the maid of honor speech in timeline form, listing the milestones of their relationship. I got to bear witness to God's goodness, His grace, the romantic little spurts and big building blocks of their relationship that I'd seen along the way. I talked about the date in 2017 when Kristen boldly and humbly told me she was praying she'd meet her husband in the next year. I shared the date when, a few months later, our friend Tyler told me he was getting ready to ask Kristen on a date in front of my house, while I watched inside from the window. I reminded them of the date they came over for a simple dinner of soup with our family, and I watched them interacting with such intimacy, knowing they'd get married.

Often, by just laying out the record, I see a testimony of the power and presence of God. I've learned through the years that you won't know how to recognize when you get what you want if you don't have a rhythm to help you recognize when you get it. So as much as I've tried to not make this about my own story, I know that we all want freedom from body shame, and I'd like to recognize that God has given it to me. So can I share some dates with you?

I was born on August 17, 1984.

In the summer of 1993, I took the car ride described in the first chapter during which I prayed to lose the "extra" parts of my body. The next few years are marked with memories of realizing that my body was not what the world deemed "good" for a little girl. There were painful pauses on playgrounds, secret shame storms I experienced in dressing rooms, and downright damaging words spoken over my body.

I was in middle school from 1995 to 1998, and I remember feeling insecure and aware that my body was a little different. For the most part, I don't remember caring too much.

High school was a different story. I started high school on my fourteenth birthday—August 17, 1998. From the very first day, I felt like my body was being measured for acceptability and desirability. I spent the first years of high school playing around with different strategies in order to be seen as both. These endeavors left me feeling broken, used, and hungry.

During my junior and senior years, things were looking up. I met Jesus! I had really amazing Christian friends, a boyfriend who loved God and loved me, and I enjoyed having fun with my friends and living what felt like a very free life. I noticed my weight creeping up but felt very little shame about it. It truly felt like something I noticed, not something I minded. What I do remember from those years is dancing with my girlfriends to Destiny's Child, reading my Bible a lot because I couldn't get enough of it, eating pizza with my boyfriend, and having the courage to teach gymnastics to little girls even though I couldn't do a cartwheel myself. I'm not sure who gave me that job, but I know it was Jesus who gave me that freedom after a few years in bondage.

During my freshman year of college, as my weight kept climbing, I noticed some ways it was impacting my health and my ability to move and keep up with my friends. This was a little concerning, but what was more concerning was how I suddenly felt very "other" than my friends. It wasn't just that our clothing sizes felt far apart, but that I had also begun to notice other people made assumptions about me that felt attached to my weight: assumptions that proclaimed I was messy, I was clumsy, I was lazy. I didn't like these assumptions or how I was living into them, but I also made a lot of assumptions in this season about how much people loved me and why they might not. I left the dorms for the summer on May 9, 2003 and made a silent promise not to return the way I was leaving.

The summer of 2003 is when things got dark for me. I was making agreements with the enemy about my worth, my value, and what made me lovable. I began trying different types of disordered eating and behavior, some that appeared socially acceptable to outsiders, and some I kept hidden because I knew they wouldn't be. My body changed, and people praised me for it.

When I came back to school in the fall, I didn't just look different—I acted different. There was no messy, clumsy, or lazy allowed in my life. I exercised twice a day, tracked every crumb that went into my body, worked a part-time job at a church off campus, and gave 110 percent in every class because I wanted to be seen as a high achiever, not as a messy girl who couldn't keep up. I was miserable and stressed but highly functioning and fueled by the praise of the people I loved.

This disordered eating and unhealthy behavior continued from 2003 until 2005, when I married that amazing high-school boyfriend—the one who had loved my body at varying sizes and shapes. My wedding day felt like an exam I was taking to finally get the stamp of approval on my body that I'd been craving compulsively for the past few years. I regret that I was distracted by focusing on my body that day, but more than that, I regret that my unhealthy behavior led me to set a bar for myself that should never have been in place. For years, I tried to get back to my wedding day weight, as if that was the pinnacle of perfection, as if it was something that could be attained without causing serious harm to my body.

From 2003 until 2014, it will be quicker for me to list short seasons when I experienced freedom or, at least, compassion for myself in regard to my body image. In between my first and second kiddos being born, I felt full in the best ways. Joyful and free. At ease and in no hurry to please anyone. The only problem was that there were only four months in between the birth of my first son and the date I got pregnant with my second—the peace was short-lived.

I decided to become a runner in the summer of 2010, to help combat my postpartum depression after my third child was born. I explored new areas of strength in myself in that season, and I spent a lot of time talking to God. I was so distracted with the defeat and despair and the havoc my hormones were wreaking on my mind and emotions, I had no energy left for body shame. With the voice of shame quieted, I began to realize that running made me feel strong and brought me a daily sense of victory.

In the spring of 2011, I experienced a miscarriage, and the shame came back, this time new and fresh, pointy and jagged in very tender places. Now, not only did I battle the sensation of being too much, too fluffy, too messy, I also felt like my body was intrinsically inadequate in a new way. I began to provoke my body again; my exercise and eating may not have looked that different from the outside, but the motivation was: withholding and perfecting, not celebrating and healing.

It was early 2014 when I sent the middle-of-the-night email to Alisa Keeton, asking her to coach me, and it was then that I began praying this prayer: *God help me want to see You more than I want to see my body fit into some culturally acceptable mold. Help me want You more than I want my body to seem good to others. Help me believe what You've said about my body.*

In the six years since then, God and I have done a lot of work. On runs, in the kitchen, in my journal. In front of mirrors, in conversations with my counselor and my girlfriends. As a true Enneagram 8, I have mostly kept this very tender part of my heart to myself, sharing it only with those I'm closest to, but I always prayed about writing the book to share the freedom that God has given me.

In the spring of 2019, I had a meeting with my publisher about my book *You Are the Girl for the Job.* The conversation meandered to future books, and I said the brave thing that was thumping in my heart: "Next, I'd like to write a body book."

On March 4, 2020 I had another meeting with my amazing editor Stephanie, just days before the coronavirus pandemic hit the United States. We talked again about a body book—about the pain points of women and what words God might give us to tell them. As I flew home from our meeting in Nashville that night, I hunched over my laptop and typed out the words of the first chapter. Nine days later, it felt like the world blew up as we began social distancing and everything stopped. I forgot about the book for a few weeks.

On April 22, Stephanie and I caught up over Zoom with the intent to talk about my next book. I told her later that I'd prayed she would have an idea for a different book—I was losing my nerve to write the body book. It was too close, too real, too much for me to be so vulnerable about. But she didn't have another idea; instead, she had only more passion for the project and invited me to "write bravely and see what happens." I wrote the words "write bravely" on a sticky note and put it on my bedside table.

My call with Stephanie was on Wednesday, I had a busy workday on Thursday, I took Friday and Saturday off, and woke up Sunday morning at 5 a.m. ready to go, ready to write. I began writing this book that day and finished the first draft of the manuscript exactly sixty days later, on June 26, 2020. Those were holy, sacred, beautiful days. I'd get done writing in the morning and think all day on the words God had given me earlier. I thought about you all every single day and prayed for you—prayed for us. I prayed for revival, and I prayed for shame to fall off of us collectively, individually, and definitively.

In July, our family went on sabbatical, and I entered what I now describe as a redeemed Eden state. Our city was in the middle of an intense COVID outbreak, so the travel we'd planned for our sabbatical turned into a quiet family staycation. We rented a beach house on a small barrier island a few miles away from our home and did nothing but spend time with our immediate family for thirty-one days. We deleted all social media, didn't bring our laptops, and rested like our lives depended on it. I took a few bathing suits and comfy dresses and a freshly printed copy of this manuscript. I was determined to read the book as if it wasn't my own, to ask myself the questions at the end of each chapter, to make sure I believed it to be true and helpful for me, as well as you.

In the mornings I read the Bible and this book, and the rest of the days I spent living free in my own body. I moved, I rested, I lived in a bathing suit like it wasn't an ensemble of shame.

Sometime during the month, I got to this question in chapter 7: *What would an act of worship in your body, outside of the typical singing and dancing, look like today?* And I wrote "become a barre instructor" in the margins of my manuscript. A year earlier, I'd begun attending a barre studio in Charleston, and I knew from my very first class that I wanted to be an instructor. The owner of the studio had even suggested I audition to be an instructor, but I only found defeat and discouragement in my heart when I considered it. I'm thirty-six. Very curvy. Not your average fitness instructor. My heart is free, but my body doesn't fit the typical fitness instructor mold.

Until I read this book and remembered that I live in the kingdom. And in the kingdom, there is not typical, there is just intentionally made. And the most worshipful thing I could do with this body is say yes to lead in a brave new space, in a brave new way. So that day, in the middle of sabbatical, I started practicing for my audition.

Around the end of sabbatical, I had a conversation with my mother and sister. They asked how my heart was doing with the book, and I relayed to them just how free I felt. My mom then told me that recently, my stepdad had said, "Jess doesn't really look different, but she looks like she *feels* beautiful." I smiled big. Both of these women mirrored back what I felt in my heart: I am free, and I am living out my freedom, and other people can see it.

It's now October 18, 2020. The air is cooler in Charleston, and yesterday I bought pumpkins for our front porch. I've taught three barre classes so far, and I teach my fourth this afternoon. It's been wild and really fun to use my body in this way. Sure, during each class I fight the lies that come about my body—but for the most part, it's incredibly worshipful to bring my whole self to the table to fight shame, condemnation, and comparison.

Yesterday I looked back at my 2020 goals, because I'm a goals gal. I had five main goals for this year, but writing a book wasn't one of them because I thought I was taking the year off from writing:

*Create space to hear from God.*
*Grow in passion in my marriage.*
*Lead my kids in love.*
*Heal my body.*
*Save for the next season.*

I was evaluating and assessing what progress had been made in all of those areas, but as I did, I noticed something interesting about the body goal. Each month, I rewrite each of my yearly goals somewhere near my monthly goals in order to remember what they are, and somewhere around June, my body goal changed.

Instead of writing "Heal my body," I wrote, "Live healed in my body," because I sensed the healing *had happened.*

Because this is a fact-based timeline, I'm here to tell you that no metrics in my body have shifted. I weigh what I weighed in March 2020, and I look roughly the same except that my hair has gotten to be ridiculously long because I've taken the pandemic as a solid excuse to stop going to the hair stylist. I still take medication for my autoimmune disorder and get Vitamin B12 shots once a month to help my energy and immunity. I'm still the size I was. I'm still me.

Except—I know I'm free. I know my body is good. I know it isn't defined by the expectations or the characteristics of this fallen world that cause it to experience pain.

I love this body. It breathes and moves and builds the kingdom of God. It grows and groans and gives great hugs. It gives me a home to experience heaven here on earth; it gives me space to be still and small when the world seems to be spinning out of control. I want it to experience the ultimate healing that is headed it's way in eternity, but I don't want to ditch this body like it's been bad all along. I want to spend the rest of my life showing gratitude and grace toward this particular body that God intentionally placed me in. I love this body.

And if I could hand you a pill or tell you to say a special prayer and feel this way, I would. I'd give it to you for free. Because I do now know that it is possible for someone who has felt the depths of pain and hatred toward her own flesh to feel grateful and filled with gratitude. But the best thing I can give you is this path that I have walked.

*Rename your body as good with God.* He called it that first. Agree with Him. Change your language, and watch the culture change around you. Speak life, and watch life mirrored back to you.

*Give your body rest from provoking it and trying to make it better.* Stop treating your body like a project to be finished and give it space to breathe. Stop trying to beat the curse, and stop requiring your body to be better. Say yes to the rest God has provided.

*Find restoration through worship.* Let your body be a place where you see God. See His grace, and also see Him bring growth. Let God change your mind about what your body can do and what it's for. Worship when you eat, drink, move, and experience your body. This is what you were made for.

*Seek revival for yourself and others.* This is what seals the healing in. I cannot genuinely want you to experience truth in your body if I'm not experiencing it myself. When we wade into the waters of repentance, intercession, and revival—when we get so deep that we're caring not just for ourselves but for others, we can't help but let the mercy of God wash over us. Don't just dip your toe into the shallows of freedom—dive in and call others to join you. Get out into the current and get carried away. This is a safe place to get swept up.

I know this path has changed my life. I know I live free in this good body. I want the same for you, too.

*If the Son has set you free, you are free indeed.*

God has purchased your freedom and prepared a path for you to walk into it.

What testimonies will you tell about your body? About the weeks and years to come? What date will you write down as the moment you began to believe and live as if your body was good?

Will it be today?

# Contributors

**Ariana** is a proud Latina and third-generation minister of the gospel. She has spent her adult life invested in the discipleship of women. Her anointing as a teacher of God's Word inspires others to pursue a transformational life with Jesus.

**Jensine** is a thirty-something Asian-American mom of two in the San Francisco Bay Area. She is a marketing gal who loves sports and books. After difficult postpartum seasons, she is learning to build physical and spiritual strength in order to mother and to minister.

**Jillana** is a singer-songwriter and recent transplant to Houston, Texas. She leads worship at her church, loves to bake, and is most comfortable with an iced coffee in hand.

**Kati** is a forty-eight-year-old wife, mother, and grandmother who lives in a body with cerebral palsy. Due to complications from major surgery in 2016 that nearly cost her mobility, she was forced to medically retire from a fifteen-year career in military service (as a civilian) that she was completely passionate about. She has spent the time since then healing and working to regain her mobility. She is currently a full-time caregiver to her grandson and a certified yoga teacher, specializing in accessible yoga and certified in kids' yoga.

**Kim** is a forty-two-year-old mother of two who lives in the northeast. She coleads her church alongside her husband. She encourages women of all ages to be rooted and grounded in who they are in Christ and to experience the freedom only He can give.

**RWP** is a forty-year-old woman who has served in East Asia as a missionary since 2008. She is a wife of seventeen years, mother of three preteen/teen boys, and proof that anyone can homeschool their children. She will help with any home or office organizing project in exchange for a cup of black coffee.

**Sarah** is a thirty-year-old physical therapist currently living in Charleston, South Carolina with her husband and their dog, Lucy.

**Tiffany** is a forty-year-old wife, mother of five, and church planter. Originally from New Jersey, Tiffany now lives in the DC metropolitan area. In her spare time, she loves teaching and taking dance classes, gathering with friends, and rocking leopard print and cat eye glasses.

**Treasure** is a single twenty-five-year-old who lives in Detroit. She attends seminary and is a self-proclaimed coffee enthusiast.

# Thank You

Listen, I'm serious: all glory to God. Thank you, Jesus! For saving my soul and rescuing me from the pit of shame, condemnation, and self-hatred. Healing, hope, freedom, and health were always Your idea, and I couldn't be more grateful.

Stephanie Smith: your commissioning is always more than I could ever ask for or imagine. The way you lead me through invitation and the masses through editing is a thing to behold.

Mom, Gibson, Rubes, Josh, and Caroline: thanks for sitting on the porch that day in April and giving me permission and encouragement to write fast, furiously, and fervently. Thanks for loving me through my own healing and for dreaming with me about this message.

Jenni Burke: you have shown up for me and for the women of God so well through your work. I am so grateful for you, and I'm so thankful we get to be the most grateful gals in publishing together.

Kristen, Britt, Hannah, Gabby, and Tiffany: you were the midwives of this particular mission, and I will be on your team forever.

Alicia Kasen: thank you for loving this book with your heart, soul, mind, and strength.

Anna, Brenna, Henslee, Caroline, and Abbey: you've always been the girls for the job. Thanks for doing the work with me.

Alisa Keeton: you're a pastor, a prophet, and a very good friend. Thank you for fighting with me and for me in the throne room of grace.

Jensine, Tiffany, Kim, Kati, Sarah, Treasure, Jillana, Ari, and

R: thank you each for sharing your stories and being a part of this project.

Glory: thanks for being the most God-confident gal I know.

Elias, Benja, and Cannon: keep being a part of the solution. The women of your generation need strong men who love and lead in freedom. That's who you are.

Nick: I don't think there's ever been a human man who has championed the true freedom of women more than you. I stand by that statement and credit so much of this work to your encouragement.

# Resources

Revelation Wellness: www.revelationwellness.org

Online Christian Counseling: www.faithfulcounseling.com

Onsite Workshops: www.onsiteworkshops.com

*The Wellness Revelation* by Alisa Keeton

# Dance, Stand, Run

## The God-Inspired Moves of a Woman on Holy Ground

*Jess Connolly*

Abundant life is within your reach. Join Jess Connolly as she casts a fresh vision for how to break free of cheap grace and empty rule-keeping and change the world rather than be changed by it. Spoiler alert: it's a beautiful thing.

Grace is always good news. But it's not cheap—true grace compels us to change, and that's where holiness comes in.

Jess Connolly—beloved writer, speaker, business coach, co-author of *Wild and Free*, and author of *You Are the Girl for the Job*—will be the first to admit that not long ago, like many women, she grasped grace but forgot about holiness. Through story and study, *Dance, Stand, Run* charts her discovery that holiness was never meant to be a shaming reminder of what we "should" do, but rather a profound privilege of becoming more like Christ.

*Dance, Stand, Run* is an invitation to the daughters of God to step into the movements of abundant life: dancing in grace, standing firm in holiness, and running on mission. Jess will help you to:

- Embrace your identity as a holy daughter of God
- Break free of cheap grace and empty rule-keeping
- Live out your holy influence with confidence before a watching world

Want to go deeper? Study guide and video study also available.

*Available in stores and online!*

**ZONDERVAN®**
.com

# Wild and Free

## A Hope-Filled Anthem for the Woman Who Feels She Is Both Too Much and Never Enough

*Jess Connolly and Hayley Morgan*

You don't have to be everything to everyone. You don't have to try so hard to button it up and hold it together. Join Jess and Hayley as they reveal how women today can walk in the true liberty we already have in Jesus.

For all the fullness of God available to His daughters, we often feel limited by two defining insecurities: "I am too much," and "I am not enough."

Coauthors and best friends Jess Connolly and Hayley Morgan have felt the same, until one essential question turned the tables on it all: If God is wild and free and He created women, what does this mean for us today?

*Wild and Free* is an anthem and an invitation in equal parts to find freedom from the cultural captivity that holds us back, and freedom to step into the wild and holy call of God in our lives. With fresh biblical insight tracing all the way back to Eve and a treasury of practical application, Jess and Hayley reveal how women today can walk in the true liberty we already have in Jesus.

Because you don't have to be everything to everyone. You don't have to try so hard to button it up and hold it together. And you certainly don't have to quiet the voice that God gave you when He created you to sing. *Wild and Free* will help you shake off the lies of insecurity in your life, and step forward to maximize your God-given influence for His glory and the world's good.

*Available in stores and online!*

# You Are the Girl for the Job

## Daring to Believe the God Who Calls You

### Jess Connolly

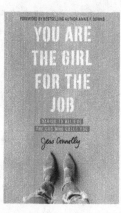

You believe (or want to believe) God has called you and given you purpose, but where do you start? How do you get from feeling stuck to making a move? If this sounds familiar, bestselling author Jess Connolly has a message for you: *You Are the Girl for the Job*.

But this is not simply a peppy catchphrase. This is the straight-up truth God has proclaimed over your life from the beginning, and it's not dependent on what you can do or achieve but based on His power, capacity, and character.

It has taken one million, maybe one zillion (who knows?!), slight moves of His hand to place you in this exact moment. So forget about fear and second-guessing your gifts, because God has meticulously prepared you to be an ambassador for the Kingdom right where you are, here and now. Life is too short to get stuck in a holding pattern of shame, self-doubt, and comparison. So let this book be your very good news: you don't have to wait for permission when you've already been commissioned.

With passion and heart-pumping hope, Jess shows that being the girl for the job doesn't depend on your capacity. Rather, it has everything to do with God's capacity and our willingness. It has everything to do with believing we are who God says we are, and quieting any inferior word spoken against us. Are you ready?

Let this book be your jump start into confident, purposed living, as Jess walks you through the six steps she has used to coach and encourage women for years: set your focus, take stock of the story that has shaped you, face your fear, catch the vision, make a plan, and finally, make your move—all in the bold belief that God has called you to every step of the journey.

Want to go deeper? Study guide and video study also available.

*Available in stores and online!*

**ZONDERVAN®**
.com